To
Shirlee

WHEN TWO WORLDS COLLIDE

Barb Engels

WHEN TWO WORLDS COLLIDE

The pundits of television and radio, friends and relatives daily feed us an endless stream of well-meaning advice in how to successfully deal with life's vicissitudes and problematic situations. We are pulled this way and that way like rudderless boats cast upon a series of huge waves caught in a tempest by whomever or whatever exerts the most influence upon us at any particular point in time. Our life has no direction, but that which is imposed upon us by events and seemingly knowledgeable people. In Barbara Engels' newest book, When Two Worlds Collide, the author through continuing the story of the Cole family dares to suggest to the reader that he 'be still'. In a world where we feverishly turn to Oprah or

WHEN TWO WORLDS COLLIDE

Dr. Laura or Dr. Phil or any other popular expert for our daily dose of advice, it is radical indeed to tell the reader to 'be still'. Engels dares to suggest that we do the unthinkable and when the ominous black clouds of a problem swirl about us that we 'be still', and let our Creator speak to us and solutions will be found. When Two Worlds Collide is excellent in that it tells a great story, but on a deeper level it makes us stop and think about our relationship to God and how through communing with Him we may bring our lives back on track.

Don M. McKay
Author/Publisher
Black Hat Publishing

WHEN TWO WORLDS COLLIDE

Barbara Engels

When Two Worlds Collide
ISBN: 1-894928-16-4

© Copyright 2003 by Barbara Engels
Millet, Alberta, Canada

All rights reserved.
This is a work of fiction. The characters and incidents in this novel are products of the author's imagination. Any resemblance to any event or any person, living or dead, is purely coincidental.

Scripture quoted from The Holy Bible, New King James Version, copyright 1982 by Thomas Nelson, Inc.

Even though it may not be grammatically correct, the author chooses not to capitalize the name of satan to give him any acknowledgement. However, all instances pertaining to the Lord Jesus Christ, God, and the Holy Spirit are all capitalized. To Him belongs all acknowledgement and glory.

Editors: Cori Van Housen
Don and Barb McKay

Cover design: John Thomson

Publisher: Barb Engels
R.R. 1
Millet, Alberta T0C 1Z0

Printed by Word Alive Press

IN LOVING MEMORY OF A
WONDERFUL FRIEND
GEORGINA HENDERSON

(ENA)

WHO GRADUATED AND WENT TO BE WITH
THE LORD OCTOBER 3, 2002

DEDICATIONS

Heavenly Father, thank you for the words You gave me to write! With You all things are possible.

I dedicate this book to Tijuana Christian Mission . . . City of Refuge, where children and adults are ministered to daily. Though the characters are fictional in the Mission . . . Tijuana Christian Mission, City of Refuge is a very real place. For more information about this ministry you can write to Martha Lopez at PO Box 85, National City, CA 91951-0085, USA. Their e-mail address is Tcmcor2@hotmail.com

ACKNOWLEDGEMENTS

It's because of your love and support Fred, that I've been able to write the sequel to Stranger Within . . . thank you! I can now make you cookies again.

To my sons Fred Jr. and Stephen . . . I love you!

To my grandson Devon . . . I love you!

To the Heimdal Community Church and the ladies bible study for all your prayers and support. Thank you for your encouragement!

Thank you Cori, Don and Barb for the hours you spent proofreading and editing my manuscript. I'm forever grateful!

Psalm 46:10

Be still, and know that I am God;
I will be exalted among the nations,
I will be exalted in the earth!

CHAPTER ONE

Dan and Belinda Cole stood on the landing of the church where a memorial service had just taken place for Clara Coburn.

"That was a wonderful service. For that old rancher to come to Christ was so exciting! Clara would have loved it, Belinda," said Dan. "She was like a Mom to me, I'm going to miss her," he added, shutting the truck door and putting his arm around Belinda's shoulder. "Too bad Peter and Stacey couldn't have been here, but knowing Clara, she would have understood."

"Well, it is kind of hard with their new baby and all to be traveling right now, Dan." Belinda then began to think about the little girl they had lost and right away thought about Joshua. He had turned out to be the best son parents could have.

WHEN TWO WORLDS COLLIDE

"Thinking about Joshua are you, Belinda? He should be home from college in a week. We'll soon have our own pastor in the family. I'm sure proud of him."

"I am too, Dan. I am too."

Clearing the dishes from supper, Belinda heard the phone ringing and wiped her hands on a dishtowel. She picked up the phone only to hear Dan's voice on the other end. A woman was insisting she needed to see them both right away.

"I don't want to explain this all over the phone, Mr. Cole, but I need to talk to you and your wife right away. It is quite urgent. I can't travel and was wondering if you wouldn't mind coming to the Applegate Nursing Home. Can I give you the address?"

"That's okay," Belinda heard Dan say, "I know where it is. Yes, we will be there as soon as we can. Bye."

Dan came into the kitchen with a puzzled look on his face. "Now, that was a strange call, Belinda."

"I know, I picked up the phone when it rang, but you reached it first. Did you hear the lady's voice tremble? She didn't sound well, did she?"

CHAPTER ONE

"I told her we would come right over, Belinda. I'll help you clean up later."

After speaking to the receptionist at the Applegate Nursing Home, and receiving directions to the woman's room, Belinda and Dan found a small form curled up under an afghan.

"Excuse me Ma'am," said Dan, putting his hand gently on her shoulder, "we don't want to bother you, but you called us earlier this evening."

The older woman slowly aroused and tried to sit up. Dan quickly helped by putting a pillow behind her, to prop her into a somewhat sitting position. "Yes, I must have dozed off. Sorry. I haven't been feeling very good, but I'm sure you don't want to hear about all my aches and pains."

Her silver hair was topsy-turvy and deep lines etched her face. She reached over and put the light on beside her bed, then opened the nightstand's drawer and retrieved a long white envelope. She placed the envelope on her lap and took a deep breath.

"I've wanted to look you up so many times over the years, but never had the courage to do so. My name is Roberta Cleveland and I was the nurse who found the baby."

At that moment Belinda wanted to hug the woman, but something stopped her.

Roberta continued. "The doctors here are telling me I don't have long to live. I really didn't want to wait so long to tell you this; it has been over twenty-two years, but I have to get this off my chest. The baby I found all those years ago was not your baby, Mrs. Cole."

"What exactly are you saying, Roberta?" questioned Belinda, not believing what she was hearing.

"I know this is probably hard for you to hear, dear, but knowing the parents of this little soul were in another country, and finding out you just lost your baby, I felt you would be the perfect match."

"Hard for me to hear! Do you know what you are saying?" Belinda stared at the woman incredulously.

Roberta glanced over to Dan looking for support. Not sensing any she closed her eyes and tried to calm her racing heart. Could it have been a mistake to reveal this

CHAPTER ONE

secret? No. She felt she must find the courage to continue. She had known right from the start this would not be easy. Roberta opened her eyes and fixed them upon Belinda. "I'm so sorry for what I have to tell you. It seemed with all that was going on back then, nobody even checked the birth records, so I forged your name on the forms. I know now this was a terrible thing to do."

"It wasn't just terrible, Roberta, it was illegal," interjected Dan.

Roberta nodded. "I know." Her hands shook as she handed him the envelope. "You will see the parents are from Alberta, Canada. After being told their baby had died, they went back home. The envelope contains the official birth papers."

"Why didn't you contact them?" asked Belinda, desperate to find some meaning to this insanity.

"The Harding name is respected and well known. I knew the baby would be looked after."

"My last name wasn't Harding, Roberta, it was Cole."

Roberta nodded wearily. "Yes, I know, but at the time you were separated and . . ."

"How did you know I was separated?"

WHEN TWO WORLDS COLLIDE

"The whole community knew you were separated from Dan, Belinda. It wasn't a secret."

Dan drew himself closer to Belinda and put his arm around her. "It's okay, that was a long time ago, and you are healed, Belinda."

"Look," sighed Roberta, "I don't want to cause any trouble, I just want to tell the truth. Joshua turned out to be a fine young man and he is happy, isn't he?"

Belinda's heart beat wildly. How could this be? She raised someone else's child? She had to get away from this woman and her lies.

"You don't want to cause trouble! I don't believe a word you are saying!" retorted Belinda angrily.

"Now dear . . ." started Roberta.

"Don't 'dear' me. I won't stay here and listen to this anymore! I'll wait for you in the truck, Dan."

Dan's heart ached. He watched Belinda escape the scene and was left staring at Roberta, who now had tears rolling down her cheeks.

"I didn't think it would turn out so badly. I knew there would be an initial shock, but I prayed you would accept the truth. This

CHAPTER ONE

sounds selfish, but I had to have peace before I died."

"You prayed, Roberta? Do you know Jesus Christ as your personal Savior?"

Roberta nodded. "A sweet nurse in here led me to the Lord. I'm so grateful to her. Then I knew I had to tell the truth. It says in the Word that the truth sets us free."

"Yes, speaking the truth will set us free. My wife has been through so much and I know eventually she will see this as truth, but she will have to process this information first. We both will."

Dan looked down at the envelope in his hands and sat down on a chair beside Roberta's bed. He opened it and typed on the form were the names, Doug and Cynthia Shriver, of Cochrane, Alberta, Canada. Dan looked at the paper again and groaned inside. *"Father, what do you want me to do?"* breathed Dan as he sought the Lord inwardly.

"Be still."

Dan nodded and stood up. He looked down at Roberta. Her eyes were closed, so he quietly left the room. Once in the hallway, Dan sighed deeply. What would this do to their family? Could this revelation bring them closer together or separate them? Dan guessed that only time would tell.

WHEN TWO WORLDS COLLIDE

Approaching the truck, Dan saw Belinda, her head bowed and her hands clutched together. Dan opened the truck door and slipped in beside her.

"I have to talk to Roberta. Can this be true, Dan?" moaned Belinda.

"We'll call our lawyer in the morning, Belinda, and have these papers checked out. But if it is true, we have to tell Joshua. No more secrets, remember?"

"I'll be right back, Dan,"

"Heavenly Father, be with Belinda as she speaks with Roberta. Let her words be Your words," prayed Dan as he watched Belinda re-enter the Applegate Nursing Home.

Belinda slipped quietly back into the room. She found Roberta in the same position, slightly propped up on the pillow, her eyes closed. She wanted to speak the angry words she had been thinking on, but now a peace settled over her. Quietly she said, "Roberta, why now? Why would you reveal this twenty-two years later?"

"Like I said, my time is short and I had to do what the Lord instructed me to do," whispered Roberta, keeping her eyes closed.

Belinda paused. "Did you once think what this could do to our family?"

CHAPTER ONE

Roberta opened her eyes and looked at Belinda. "I'm sorry for keeping this from you, but I was afraid. I did not want to go to prison. The other nurses involved with this scam were in there for several years. I also heard the Harding's were Christians and I felt Joshua would receive a wonderful upbringing."

"Do you know God?"

"Yes I do, dear. I told your husband I received the Lord when a nurse here prayed for me. That's why I had to finally tell the truth. I've been fighting with this secret for all these years and finally I surrendered my will to His. It feels like a great burden has been lifted from my soul. I pray you will find peace in your heart about this too, Belinda. Please forgive me for not talking to you sooner."

Belinda was thankful Roberta knew the Lord, but the situation at hand was so surreal. "This is so unfair, Roberta. I've been through so much with Joshua, and I have believed all these years that he was my son. Now you're telling me he's not. How can this be?"

"I'm so sorry; I don't have all the answers. I just did what I thought was best at the time. He was such a cute little guy that I just couldn't let them put him into foster care."

"Why didn't you try to locate his birth parents?"

"If I did, an investigation would have arisen and for sure I would have been in trouble for hiding the baby in the first place. Like I said before, the Harding name is well-known and respected. I knew he would be safe. Your step-mom was so excited when I called; it seemed the right thing to do. And knowing the birth parents were in Canada, and all that distance between us, I didn't think anyone would check the validity of the papers.

Belinda thought back about Mabel. It was true, Mabel had been ecstatic over finding out Joshua was alive. Belinda sighed heavily. She tried not to let the anger strangle her again, so she reached out and took Roberta's hand. "I forgive you."

Roberta smiled. Light seemed to shine from her face, and she shut her eyes once again.

CHAPTER TWO

Dan found out Doug Shriver was a rancher near a small town west of Calgary, Alberta. So, what Roberta had shared with them about this couple was the truth. He also knew they would both have to tell Joshua, but wanted to wait until he came home from seminary. Joshua had grown so much in the Lord and they prayed the Lord would prepare him for this shocking news. It would take some time for the revelation to settle into their hearts, but meanwhile they would trust the Lord to work it out.

Joshua Cole held the certificate in his hand and looked heavenward. *"Thank you, Lord, for helping me complete these four*

years of school. I'm ready and willing to do all that You would have me do. Thank you for Mom and Dad; I know their prayers saw me through the pressures of seminary. I ask for Your protection as I travel home."

Joshua stopped his truck at the driveway leading home. He opened his window and breathed in the cool mountain air. No more walls . . . it was good to be home! He noticed the spring work had begun and he could hardly wait to get on board a tractor and see all the furrows following neatly behind him. He was still waiting for a call from the Lord, not knowing where his first assignment would take him. But for now, he was content to stay and help his mom and dad until the call came. Joshua hoped to surprise Dan and Belinda, for they weren't expecting him until sometime next week. Joshua didn't wait around for all the celebrations at school; he just wanted to get home.

"Dan, you sure are home early," called Belinda from the bedroom, when she heard the back door shut. "I was sure that south quarter would take you all day!"

Joshua quietly tiptoed down the hall and peeked around the corner at the doorway of the last bedroom. His mom was

CHAPTER TWO

fluffing the pillows. The look on her face, when she turned around, was worth it all.

"Joshua!" Belinda couldn't get to the form in the doorway fast enough. Joshua picked her up in a bear hug and twirled her around the room.

"I've missed you too, Mom!"

Joshua finally set her down and gazed down into her face. "It's so good to be home!"

"You weren't suppose to be home until next week," said Belinda, somewhat perplexed. "Nothing is wrong, is it?"

"Nope. I didn't call cause I wanted to surprise you." Joshua took a paper from his jacket and handed it to Belinda. "Your degree, Josh. When was the ceremony? Why didn't you invite us to come?"

"Hey, settle down, Mom. I didn't want to get into all the celebrations; I just sensed a need to come home. I knew Dad would be busy with the spring work around here and I wanted to help. I haven't had a definite call from the Lord yet and until I do, this is where I want to be."

"Oh, Joshua, I'm so proud of you and so is Dad!"

Joshua hugged her again. "Thank you, Mom. I know it was on account of your prayers and Dad's, that I was able to make it through. Now, what quarter is Dad in? I'm going to change and get out there. Could you make me a lunch first? I didn't stop to eat."

"Sure, Josh. I'll make you some sandwiches and Dad could use some coffee about now too."

While preparing the lunch for Joshua, Belinda lifted her voice quietly to the Lord. *"Please give Dan and I the right words to speak to Joshua about his birth parents. I don't want to lose him, but I have given him to You and I know You will look after this situation. Thank you for bringing him home safely."*

Joshua looked intently at Belinda while he sipped some coffee.

"Is something wrong, Mom?"

"No, why do you ask?"

"You could never hide your emotions, Mom. You're like an open book. Is there something you need to tell me?"

Belinda's heart began to race. "Yes, there are a few things on my mind Josh, but let's wait until supper tonight. We can talk then when we're all together."

"Okay, I better be going. Thanks for lunch."

CHAPTER TWO

Belinda watched Joshua climb into his truck and commanded her heart to slow down. Josh was so perceptive it sometimes scared her. It was almost like he could read her thoughts. She didn't control her emotions well, an area in her life where she asked the Lord to help her daily. Belinda looked at the clock above the stove. The children from the centre would soon be here and she still had the horses to saddle. She had thought about asking Joshua to stay and help her, but his eagerness to see Dan kept her silent. Excitement filled her just thinking about the children coming. With their disabilities and the horses' willingness, this made a wonderful remedy for their little souls.

Tacking up the last horse, Belinda watched as the bus pulled into the yard. She patted a horse's neck and went to greet the children.

"Belinda, the children are so excited today. They must feel spring in the air," exclaimed Susan Anderson, the director of the centre.

Belinda took Susan's outstretched hand and smiled in agreement. "Yes, there is something in the air!"

The driver was busy at the back of the bus unloading his passengers. The volunteers

WHEN TWO WORLDS COLLIDE

proceeded to push the wheelchairs carrying the children towards the outdoor arena. Laughter and squeals of delight rang out as the children saw their horses waiting for them. Each child was assigned to the same horse each week so horse and rider bonded.

Once all the children were sitting on their horses, and the volunteers were in their places . . . one standing beside them and the other ready to lead, Belinda gave them the go-ahead to begin. Belinda joined Susan who stood beside the wheelchair of one reluctant participant. "Won't you at least give it a try, Madison? Your mom said you used to ride and loved horses," reasoned Susan.

"Quit bugging me, Mrs. Anderson. I won't get on one of those nags and that's the end of it! I told you I didn't want to come here!"

"Well, if you're that unhappy, Madison, you can at least be happy for the other children," scolded Susan, moving away from Madison. "Enjoy the sunshine then."

Belinda and Susan left Madison on the outside and walked into the arena.

"We're so encouraged, Belinda. After only one month these children's motor skills have really improved. It's like they are

CHAPTER TWO

eager to try new things. We are so thankful for your participation in the program. Many on the board didn't agree with this kind of therapy at first, but seeing the change in these children has changed their minds. If only Madison would participate," said Susan, looking over at Madison. "She is such an angry girl. The doctor says she has some movement, but not using those muscles could make her lose them too."

Their attention was then drawn back to the children enjoying their mounts.

Joshua drove into the yard and noticed all the activity in the arena. His dad was just finishing up before coming in for an early supper, so Joshua thought he would come back and take a horse out for a short ride. Empty wheelchairs were lined up outside the fence, but a young woman was still sitting in one. Joshua strolled over and squatted down beside her.

"So, what are you doing out here?"

Startled, Madison jumped, looking over at the stranger.

"Sorry, didn't mean to startle you. Looks like fun in there. Why don't you join in?"

She still didn't answer, so Joshua spoke up again. "I think I know what the problem

WHEN TWO WORLDS COLLIDE

is. These are just ponies and you're probably ready for a bigger horse. Come on, I'll show you something." Joshua didn't wait for an answer; he stood behind the wheelchair and began pushing it towards the barn.

"Hey, just a minute Mister, I'm not going anywhere with you!"

By this time, amid all the protests, Joshua had pushed Madison in front of Brandy's stall. He left the girl and opened the stall gate. Brandy neighed softly and pushed her nose into Joshua's jacket. "Sorry girl, no crunchies today. But I did bring someone for you to meet. This is . . ."

"Madison, my name is Madison Linden. I don't want to be here."

"Are you afraid? Brandy won't hurt you, will you girl?" Joshua scratched a spot behind the horse's ear.

"I'm not afraid."

"Okay then, that's half the battle. Come on in. Back up a little Brandy and let the young lady in."

Madison wheeled her chair closer and put out her hand to Brandy. Brandy bent her head and Madison stroked her forehead. "She's very pretty."

"Yes, she is a nice mare. She belongs to my mom. They've won many a ribbon

CHAPTER TWO

together. By the way my name is Joshua." He extended his hand to her.

"I haven't seen you around here before," said Madison, taking his hand and then quickly letting it go.

"That's because I've been away at school."

"You can't go to a school here?"

Joshua smiled. "I was going to a Bible college."

"You're a preacher?"

"I will be as soon as I'm ordained. So, did you want me to lift you up on Brandy?"

"No, I don't want to sit up there," said Madison, shrinking back from Brandy and Joshua.

"Okay, may be another time, then. Have you always been in a wheelchair?" Joshua asked, shutting the gate and letting Brandy stick her head over.

"No."

"Do you want to tell me about it?" Joshua asked quizzing her. Joshua pulled up a bale and sat in front of her.

"Not really. But if you must know, I had an accident with my horse."

Joshua looked intently at her, "I'm sorry Madison. I shouldn't have pried."

Madison stared back at him. He seemed to care and she wondered why.

WHEN TWO WORLDS COLLIDE

"Is that why you don't want to ride anymore?" Joshua pulled a piece of hay from the bale and chewed on it, waiting for Madison to reply.

"I won't be able to ride like I use to, so what's the point? These legs are useless."

"I think you should try, Madison. You don't know what you can do unless you give it a shot. Wouldn't you just like to sit on Brandy?"

Madison suddenly felt afraid. How could she get out of this one?

"Look, she can't go anywhere in the stall and I'll be right beside you," pressed Joshua. "What do you say?"

"Well . . ."

Just then Madison heard her name being called.

"I have to go. Thanks for the offer though."

"I'll go talk to them and see if we can take you home."

Joshua was gone before Madison could object. She picked at the bale too wondering how to escape.

Joshua returned. "You have to go back with the bus, something to do with their policy. The more time you spend with horses, you will be able to gain your confidence back. I'd like you to come over sometime."

CHAPTER TWO

"I'll have to check with my mom."

"Great, I hope to hear from you soon."

Joshua pushed her to the bus. All the other children were inside and the driver lowered the ramp for Madison's chair. Once inside, Madison looked out the window to see Joshua wave goodbye. She shyly waved back.

Belinda joined Joshua and put an arm around his waist as they walked back into the arena. After untacking all the horses and putting them out to pasture, they went back to the house.

"It's so good to have you home, Joshua."

"I feel the same way, Mom. You have no idea how hard it was to stay in those classrooms when I just wanted to be outdoors. I sense the Lord isn't calling me to a church building, but to those who never go there. A fire is burning in my heart, like something drastic is going to change me. Have any ideas, Mom?"

Just then Dan came in the back door and smiled at his wife and son. "You two look so intense. What's up?"

"How come you're in so early, Dan? Thought you wanted to finish the south quarter," commented Belinda, trying to put off Joshua's earlier question.

"It'll be there tomorrow. Besides, Josh is home and I'd like to spend some time with him."

Joshua eyed them both suspiciously. Something was going on. He could sense some tenseness, especially with his mom.

"I'll get supper started," suggested Belinda.

"You're not cooking tonight, Belinda. I'm taking you both out to celebrate Josh's homecoming. First I'll need to freshen up."

Belinda followed Dan. Once in their bedroom, Dan kissed Belinda lightly on her lips. "It will be all right. Our son has grown in the Lord and the news will only draw him closer. Don't think negative about this, let's try and leave it in the Lord's hands."

"I'm trying to leave it with the Lord, but . . ."

Dan put a finger on Belinda's lips. "Try to keep from saying anything, Belinda. We both know how powerful spoken words are."

Belinda thought for a moment how over the years her words had been very detrimental to her health and well-being. Even though she was aching to say something, she decided to be still. Sensing a supernatural peace flow through her at that precise moment, she felt the Lord wanted her to be still too.

CHAPTER TWO

Back in his own room, the stirring in Joshua's heart only intensified. "*What is it Lord?*"

Not hearing an answer, Joshua changed and then started unpacking his clothes.

CHAPTER THREE

Joshua leaned back into the booth and smiled. "That was the best steak dinner I've had in a long time. Thanks, you two."

"Joshua, you're welcome. Your Mom and I are really proud of you. You stuck to your programs and now, with God's help, He will lead you on to the next phase in your life." Dan paused and looked at Belinda, who gave him a slight nod to continue. "We had an unsettling call the other day. A woman called saying she was Roberta Cleveland. She's in the Applegate Nursing Home."

The burning in Joshua's heart began to make him uncomfortable and he leaned closer to the table.

"So, what did she have to say?"

Dan reached over and took Belinda's hand. "She informed us that your mom did have a baby when you were born Joshua, but that you did not belong to her. She claims that your birth parents are from Canada. Roberta says that Belinda's son died and because she knew the Hardings were an upstanding family, she picked your mom to raise you."

Joshua heard the words, but just couldn't believe he was hearing right. He almost began to tremble.

"Come on, you guys, this is like déjà vu. We had this go-around when I was a kid. I know you aren't my natural father," said Joshua, directing his statement to Dan, "but you raised me, so you are my dad. And Mom, come on, you'll always be my mom. I don't care what this woman said."

"Dad is telling you the truth, Josh. We said we would never keep anything from you again, so when we found this out a couple of days ago, we agreed to tell you as soon as you came home." Tears collected in Belinda's eyes as she looked at Joshua struggling with the devastating news.

Joshua closed his eyes and took a deep breath. Opening his eyes, he whispered, "I need to see Roberta Cleveland."

Dan and Belinda nodded. After paying the bill, the Coles made their way to the Applegate Nursing Home.

CHAPTER THREE

The lady at the desk hesitated, shuffled through some papers, and looking up at them asked, "Are you family?"

"No," answered Dan, "we just met the lady, but my son would like to speak to her."

"I'm sorry, she died last night. She was a lonely woman; no one ever came to see her. Guess the government will have to pay for her funeral. Just doesn't seem right."

Joshua pushed his hands into his jacket pockets and approached her desk. "Ma'am, we will finance the funeral so she has a proper burial."

"She did leave a letter for a Joshua Cole, is that you?"

"Yes." Joshua took the envelope and put it inside his jacket. "Where is she now?"

"We have a funeral home adjacent to us. She's over there."

"Thank you for your help. Mom, Dad, let's go," Joshua said to his startled parents.

Outside, Dan and Belinda reached for Josh and hugged him close. "We are proud of you son. You did the right thing," whispered Dan.

Joshua Cole stood at the podium of the small country church and looked over at a

WHEN TWO WORLDS COLLIDE

table where a picture of Roberta sat and a small wooden box containing her ashes.

"I never met you on this side, Roberta, but I hope to meet you when I get home."

Joshua now looked over at the few people attending the service. **"Precious in the sight of the Lord is the death of His saints.[1]"** Joshua bowed his head. *"Father, we commit Roberta Cleveland into Your hands. She is Your daughter and according to her letter, she loved You with all of her heart. As we all do, we make mistakes and take wrong pathways, but we are so grateful for Your mercy and grace. Thank you for Your forgiveness. Thank you for sending Your Son so we have a way back to You."*

Joshua once again looked over the small gathering. "Life here on earth is very short, for once this body dies, we have a spiritual body which will live forever. The question is, where will we spend eternity? The truth is the way to eternity is either through Jesus Christ or satan; you have the choice. I pray you will choose Jesus Christ, for He is the Way, the Truth and the Life. Roberta said she had only met Him a few months ago, but she is with Him today. So, it's a time to celebrate Roberta's life, and if you are a Christian, you will see her again."

[1] Psalm 116:15

CHAPTER THREE

Joshua left the podium and placed a rose on the table beside her picture. "If anyone wants to say anything, please come forward at this time."

A woman left her pew and came to the front. "It was very difficult to be around Roberta, for she was bitter and hard to get along with. But after she gave her life to Jesus Christ, the change in her was drastic. I'm one of her nurses who looked after her. The change in her was sincere and she was a blessing to me." The woman's voice trembled, "I will miss her." She then placed her fingers to her lips and then placed them on the picture. "Goodbye, dear friend," she whispered.

After the woman went back to her seat, Pastor Kenneth Blair came and stood with Joshua. "It's sad that one of Joshua's first duties as a pastor, is to conduct this funeral. His official ordination will take place next week, so that's why I'm here today. I didn't know Roberta either, but because of her relationship with Jesus Christ, she will have everlasting life."

At the graveside, Joshua thumbed through his Bible until he found a scripture and began to read, ***"For we know that if our earthly house, this tent, is destroyed,***

WHEN TWO WORLDS COLLIDE

we have a building from God, a house not made with hands, eternal in the heavens. For in this we groan, earnestly desiring to be clothed with our habitation which is from heaven, if indeed, having been clothed, we shall not be found naked. For we who are in this tent groan, being burdened, not because we want to be unclothed, but further clothed, that mortality may be swallowed up by life. Now He who has prepared us for this very thing is God, who also has given us the Spirit as a guarantee. So we are always confident, knowing that while we are at home in the body we are absent from the Lord. For we walk by faith, not by sight. We are confident, yes, well pleased rather to be absent from the body and to be present with the Lord.[2]"

Joshua bowed his head in silence. After a few moments, he lifted his head and moved away from the graveside. Dan and Belinda moved to stand beside him. "That was a fine service, Josh," commended Dan, "you're going to be a wonderful pastor."

Joshua smiled. "Thanks Dad, I was kind of nervous; hope it didn't show."

Belinda put an arm around Joshua's waist. "No, it didn't look like you were nerv-

[2] II Corinthians 5:1-8

CHAPTER THREE

ous at all. You looked so comfortable at the podium." Belinda's face beamed with pride.

Ken Blair came over and stood with them. "Yes," agreed Ken, "it was a nice service, Joshua. I'll have your papers in order and we can ordain you sometime next week. Is this all right with you?"

"That will be fine, Pastor Blair, and thanks for being here today. I did need you to sign the papers for the funeral home."

Ken Blair smiled. "No problem, I'll see you next week."

"I was just wondering about the letter Roberta left for you," said Belinda, after Pastor Blair left.

"I'll tell you about it when we get home." Joshua glanced over at the woman who spoke on Roberta's behalf. "Let me just have a few words with that woman. Wait for me, would you?"

Making their way to the truck, Dan sensed Belinda's nervousness. "Everything will be all right. We've trusted the Lord with everything pertaining to Joshua, so I know God will bring good out of this situation, Belinda."

"I know Dan. I just don't want Joshua to be hurt. I still have a hard time believing what Roberta said, but a dying woman isn't going to lie to us, is she? I wish she hadn't have told us at all. He is our son and nobody can tell me any differently."

Dan drew Belinda close to himself. "I feel the same way, Belinda, but there has to be a reason this was revealed now. We'll deal with it through prayer and let Joshua deal with it in his way. I agree, Belinda, Joshua will always be our son."

On the drive home, Joshua was quiet, so Belinda and Dan kept quiet too. Once in the kitchen, Joshua settled himself in a chair beside the telephone. He dialed Lindens' number and Madison picked up on the other end.

"Hi, this is Joshua. Would you like to come over for an hour or so this evening?"

"Just a sec, I'll ask Mom."

Joshua could hear muffled voices in the background and then a clear voice. "Yes, she says that would be all right. Mom will bring me over." Madison paused, "I'm a bit scared. I haven't been on a horse since my accident. I don't want to chicken out, but I'm afraid."

"That's okay Madison. We all get scared sometimes, but I'll be there right beside you."

The sound of Joshua's voiced seemed

CHAPTER THREE

to soothe her and she replied, "We'll be there in an hour."

"See you then." Joshua hung up the phone and looked over at his parents looking at him. "Can you give me a hand with Madison when she gets here, Mom?"

"Is that the girl who wouldn't get involved with the program the other day?"

Joshua nodded.

"Are you sure it's a good idea we get involved with her?"

"I think she needs some one-on-one encouragement and I also think Brandy would be the horse for her. You don't mind if I use Brandy, do you?"

Belinda was silent for a moment and then answered, "I think it's great you want to help Madison. And yes, I will give you a hand, but Dad and I would really like to talk to you first. We would like to know what Roberta said in the letter she left for you."

Joshua walked back over to kitchen table and sat down sighing heavily. "This is how I'm processing the information." Joshua fixed his eyes on Dan and Belinda. "It doesn't matter who birthed me, you're my parents and no one can change that, not a piece of paper and no document on this planet can change that fact. And the woman who supposedly gave birth to me has had the same time frame as we have. Has she called to confirm it one way or the other? Even if she had, Mom, you will always be my mother. You're the ones who have been with me through all my trials. The letter Roberta left says all the things you have already said. She said she was sorry and asked for my forgiveness. She wanted to lift the weight of the burden before she died. That's why she needed to speak the truth about my birth. She did wonder if she had done the right thing about giving me to you, but after she did some checking, she knew you were the right choice. I love you both very much. I know she made the right choice. I may want to meet these people one day, but I will not pursue any contact with them, unless of course they want to meet me. My plans are to stay here on the ranch until I get a specific calling from the Lord, if that's all right with both of you."

Tears spilled under Belinda's eyelids and ran freely down her cheeks. She wasn't losing her son!

"Oh yes, Joshua! This is your home and you can stay as long as you want," cried Belinda.

CHAPTER THREE

Dan agreed. "I can always use an extra hand." Seeing the look on Belinda's face, he smiled and added, "I'm glad you chose us too, Josh. You'll always be my son."

CHAPTER FOUR

An hour later, the van drove into the yard. Joshua helped Joan Linden remove her daughter, even though Joan was quite capable of handling Madison herself. It had been almost two years since the accident, turning the Linden's lives upside down. Over time it became routine, handling Madison, but today Joan felt quite weary. Belinda noticed this and invited Joan in for a coffee. Dan excused himself, saying he had business with his foreman.

"Thanks, Belinda, that would be nice." Joan turned to Joshua. "Will you be all right with Madison?"

Joshua was already pushing Madison's chair towards the barn. He stopped when he heard Joan Linden's voice. "Yes, Ma'am, Madison and I will do just fine, won't we?"

WHEN TWO WORLDS COLLIDE

Madison looked up at Joshua and nodded slightly. She was not sure how she would react near the horse, but hoped she would not lose her nerve.

"I'll bring her back in an hour or so. If you need us, we'll be in the barn." Joshua started pushing again and soon they were in front of Brandy's stall. The horse stuck its head out and whinnied softly.

"Hey there, girl, brought you a visitor. Remember, Madison? You met her the other day. You two get know each other and I'll be right back." Joshua then disappeared into a tack room.

Madison stared up at the horse and her heart started pounding. Brandy stretched her head out looking for crunchies and Madison, not wanting to be this close, quickly wheeled back. The sudden movement startled Brandy and she jumped back. The ruckus caused Joshua to stick his head out of the tack room. "Everything all right out there, Madison?"

"Yeah."

"I'll be right there, just looking for the right bridle, has to be in here somewhere."

Madison cautiously moved back to the stall. "It's okay girl, didn't mean to scare you. I'm kind of scared, but I won't hurt you," she said softly.

CHAPTER FOUR

Brandy stuck her head out once again. Madison reached up and gently stroked her protruding nose. Madison noticed a sack of what looked like horse crunchies near another stall. She wheeled her chair toward them and put a couple of handfuls on her lap. Brandy whinnied softly when Madison came back to her stall.

When Joshua returned, Madison and Brandy were getting to know each other. Brandy was chewing contently on the crunchies and Madison was stroking the horse's face, the gate keeping them from getting too close.

"I see you've found her favorite treat."

"Hope that's okay, Mr. Cole."

"Sure, and why don't you just call me Joshua?"

"Oh, I couldn't do that, Mr. Cole. It wouldn't seem proper." Madison thought for a moment, "How about P.J.?"

"P.J.?"

"Well, P. for pastor and J. for Joshua."

Joshua smiled. "That sounds good, Madison."

Madison moved away from the entrance as Joshua went in and placed a bridle on Brandy. Once the horse was out of the stall, fear caused Madison to tremble.

WHEN TWO WORLDS COLLIDE

Her heart started to pound and she could hardly breathe.

"Okay, Madison. You lead her and I'll push you."

"I don't think I can Mr. . . . I mean P.J."

"Sure you can. I'll be right here, and nothing will happen. Brandy knows how to behave herself, don't you girl," said Joshua, stroking the horse's neck.

Joshua handed the reins to Madison. "I'll be right here. Let's take her into the arena. That way if she shies or anything, she won't go anywhere."

"I thought you just said nothing could happen."

"Well, as you know, horses are flight animals, so we're being cautious is all."

Madison felt an enormous lump in her throat and she hoped her heart would not stop beating. Her hands felt sweaty as she looked up at Brandy, a giant of a horse alongside a chair. She gripped the reins tightly so Joshua wouldn't notice her trembling hands. But Brandy was minding her manners and walked alongside Madison.

"Good," encouraged Joshua, "you're doing great! Okay, lets speed up just a bit."

In a few strides, Brandy had now picked up her pace. All fear seemed to subside

CHAPTER FOUR

and Madison felt everything would be all right. It was so thrilling to be close to the love of her life . . . horses. Madison wished she could turn back the hands of time. This time she would have worn her helmet during her jump-off. Her disobedience had put her into a wheelchair.

"I've had enough today," Madison said suddenly.

Joshua stopped pushing her and took Brandy to the fence. He tied Brandy and went back to squat in front of Madison. "You did really well. You're facing the fear of being hurt, and it won't be long until you are riding like a pro again."

Madison shook her head. "They said I would never ride again."

"I don't believe that, Madison. My mom told me you have some movement, but if you don't begin using those muscles, you'll lose them completely. Let's just take one step at a time and see what happens."

Madison suddenly turned on Joshua angrily, "You're the one who doesn't get it! I can never take a step . . . do you hear me? I'll be in this chair for the rest of my life!"

Joshua ignored her outburst, "I'm praying for you, Madison. I believe in the power of prayer. I've seen people healed. Nothing is too hard for God."

WHEN TWO WORLDS COLLIDE

"Well, I don't believe in God anymore!"

"God still believes in you, Madison." Joshua didn't wait for a reply as he pushed her to the van. "I'll get your mom."

Joshua found Joan and his mom staring out the kitchen window.

"That's the closest Madison has been to a horse in two years, Joshua," said Joan encouraged at what she had witnessed.

"This isn't going to be easy, Mrs. Linden. Madison is very angry and bitter about living in her chair, but with God's help, I believe she will ride again. Do you believe in God?"

"Yes, I do Joshua. If it wasn't for Him I don't know how I could cope with everything we have to go through day by day. Your mom and I were just talking about this very thing before you came in. She shared about her miracle of being healed. Do you think Madison can be healed?"

"It's written in God's word that if two agree as touching anything here on earth, then it will be done for them by their Father in heaven. Yes, I believe Madison can be healed," replied Joshua with assurance.

"When Madison was first hurt, we had Pastor Blair come and pray for her, but I don't think he believes in healing here on earth. I'm just learning about the prayers of

CHAPTER FOUR

agreement, so if you can agree with my husband and myself, we sure would appreciate it. I've been praying for her to rededicate her life to the Lord."

"She knows the Lord, then?" asked Joshua puzzled by her statement. "I told Madison I would be praying for her."

"What did she say?" asked Joan, surprised by Joshua's boldness.

"She didn't say anything. She wasn't going to admit to anything, I guess. I left her over by the van. I think she's had enough for one day. It would be great if Madison could come every two weeks, but only if it's her decision. I don't want to force her into anything."

"Hey, look, you two," said Belinda, turning to the kitchen window once again.

There was Madison, wheeled up to the fence and petting Brandy.

Joan reached for Joshua's hand, "Thank you so much for helping with Madison. I'm sure you can count on Madison's full co-operation."

"You're welcome, Mrs. Linden. See you in a couple of weeks. I'll come out and give you a hand with Madison."

"No, that's okay. It's easier for some reason getting her into the van. Bye for now."

WHEN TWO WORLDS COLLIDE

Belinda and Joshua watched as Joan assisted her daughter and drove off.

"Joan sure has her hands full with that girl," said Belinda, opening the fridge door. "Joan told me some of the obstacles she faces daily. Seems Madison has quite a temper, so we need to keep in prayer for the whole family."

"Yeah, I witnessed some of that anger a little while ago."

Belinda shut the fridge door, and placed the salad ingredients on the counter. "Why, what happened?"

"Everything seemed to be going okay, when Madison abruptly stopped and wanted to go home. I think she was thinking about her accident. I told her we would just take a step at a time and she exploded. May be a wrong choice of words, but when I didn't react, I think it made her angrier. You can be praying for me too. I'll need patience."

Just then the phone rang and Belinda picked it up.

"Hello. Yes, Joshua is here, Pastor Blair. Just a moment, please."

Belinda handed the phone to Joshua.

"Hello."

"Welcome home Joshua! I didn't think it was appropriate to say this at the funeral."

CHAPTER FOUR

"Thanks, it's really good to be home."

"I was wondering if you could come down to the church tomorrow morning, say around 10:00 a.m.? I would like to talk to you about your ordination and some other pressing matters."

"Sure, I'll be there. Bye."

After hanging up the phone, Joshua poured himself a cup of coffee. "Hmm, wonder what other pressing matters Pastor Blair is talking about?"

"I thought he didn't need to see you until next week."

"That's what I thought too, but I'm to meet him tomorrow morning."

Dan came through the door. "Who are you meeting at the church?"

"Pastor Blair. He wants to see me tomorrow morning. Can you spare me for a few hours?"

"Sure Josh," said Dan pouring himself a coffee and joining Belinda and Josh at the table. "Tyler and I were just talking about scheduling for the next couple of months. We're going to be gone about four days to check on the new mamas and tag the babies."

"Tyler Blackburn? I thought you didn't like the guy."

WHEN TWO WORLDS COLLIDE

"Well, he did seem pretty young to be a foreman and a little wild for my taste, but he settled down and is a very hard worker. I think the Lord had something to do with the way he turned around." Dan smiled at Belinda. "Your mom lead him to the Lord."

"Really, Mom. I didn't know!"

"He kept asking me questions about the bar brawl those many years ago between your dad and Russ Jacobs," reminisced Belinda. "I told him the story and later found out he had also talked to Russ. So, one day when he was doing some things around the yard, he came to the house to talk. After some discussion, he asked Jesus into his heart."

"With Tyler on our side, there won't be a hand here not serving the Lord. He can be quite determined."

Dan chuckled. "You're right about that."

"I really want to help with new babies. May be I could come out as soon as I'm finished with Pastor Blair," said Joshua.

"I have a feeling Pastor Blair may need you right away, Josh. He's been looking pretty run down lately."

"Are you thinking he wants me to help on Sundays? He didn't look too bad at the funeral though," observed Joshua.

CHAPTER FOUR

"I don't know, Josh, just a sensing I get."

"You're right Dan," added Belinda, "he hasn't been the same since Alice passed away."

"Well, guess I'll wait and see what he has to say. This is only Tuesday, so I could still come out for a couple of days."

"Suit yourself Josh, we can always use an extra hand."

"Like I said before," Joshua said, "it's nice to be home."

CHAPTER FIVE

Ken Blair looked up from a stack of papers on his desk when Joshua was ushered in. Standing, he extended his hand to Joshua.

"Nice of you to come, Joshua."

The secretary left them and went back to her office. Joshua took his hand and shook it firmly. "You sounded like it was urgent, Pastor Blair."

Ken wearily sat down and Joshua took the chair across from him. "Call me Ken, please."

"How about I call you Pastor Ken?"

Ken just nodded and stared at the pile of papers. He then closed his eyes and sighed. "I'm not sure," he started, slowly opening his eyes, "how to put this, but I'm just so tired. Every little thing lately weighs heavily on my heart. This flock the Lord asked me to shepherd is too much responsibility. I need to get away. I don't hear God's voice anymore and the flock is restless. In the last couple of months, three families have left the church and I can't blame them. I don't remember how things got so out of hand."

Joshua was listening and studying his pastor of several years. He knew the answer was in seeking and spending time with the Lord, but he was sure Pastor Blair did this.

Ken continued. "I know you're just fresh out of school and this may be too much to ask of you, but would you consider taking over the services for a while?"

Joshua, deep in thought, did not answer.

"Joshua? Did you hear what I just asked you?"

"Yes, Pastor Blair, I mean Pastor Ken, how long would this arrangement be for?"

"I'm not sure. Could be a couple of weeks, could be for two months. After we have your ordination ceremony, I would like you to take the services for me. I've talked this over with the elders and they're in agreement. We just haven't talked about my replacement yet."

"Will that be a problem?"

"They know you have been keeping in

CHAPTER FIVE

touch with me while you were at Bible College, although they might think you are a little young for so much responsibility, but I think you're the best man for the job. After all, you know so many of the people, and besides, not too many pastors out there like a small rural church. I'll speak with the elders and then after your ordination, I'll take the time off."

"Had you thought of a place to rest and get the solitude you need?"

"No, Joshua, but all I know is, I need to get away."

"Would you consider going up to the hunting cabin on our property?"

"Thanks, sounds like a good idea. No one will bother me up there, will they? Ever since Alice went on to be with the Lord, I just can't seem to get anything together."

"It's been over a year now, hasn't it?"

"Yes, it will be a year and one week tomorrow. I miss her."

Joshua shifted in his seat. "Pastor Ken, I'll look after the services for you. After my ceremony, come to the ranch and we'll look after the provisions so you can go to the cabin."

"Before I go up there, I'd like to do a little fishing."

WHEN TWO WORLDS COLLIDE

"Fishing? We have the best stream not far from the cabin. In fact, they leap right out of the water practically in front of you."

Ken smiled. "Now, that's the best fish story I've heard in a long time."

Joshua smiled back. "What I guess I mean is, there is fish in the stream. Mom will take you up there in the helicopter and it would be just a short hike up to the cabin. She still has her license."

"Your mom is quite the lady, Joshua. She's been a Godsend to me after Alice died. Belinda seemed to know just when I needed a casserole, a hug, or just a listening ear."

Joshua smiled. Yup, that was his mom all right, he thought to himself.

Making his mind up, Ken said, "You talked me into it, Joshua. I'll be ready to go after your ordination ceremony. You can use my office while I'm away."

"Thanks, Pastor Ken. I'm at the ranch unless people want to reach me. I seem to hear the Lord better astride my horse or walking the land."

Hearing this made Ken chuckle to himself. Oh, to be young and eager for the voice of the Lord once again. He couldn't recall the last time the Lord had spoken

CHAPTER FIVE

clearly to him. He had distanced himself from God after Alice passed away. He wanted a miracle that never came. Alice had looked to him for support and prayer. Ken sighed heavily and looked at Joshua. Such peace he perceived there.

"If we're through here, Pastor Ken, I'm going to look for Dad and the boys. They're checking on the new mamas and babies. I'll see you Sunday." Joshua stood up and extended his hand.

Ken stood and took Joshua's outstretched hand. "Thanks Joshua, I knew I could count on you. I'll talk to the board, and see you Sunday."

Joshua tied his sleeping bag to the back of the saddle. This would be great, thought Joshua, after being in studies for four years, sleeping under the stars and riding with the boys was just what he needed. He would have to remember his Bible and notebook. He was sure he would get a message from the Lord.

"Joshua," called Belinda from the back door, "don't forget your saddlebags!"

Joshua smiled. His mom was still the mother hen looking after her chick. "I wasn't planning on fasting, Mom, I'll be right there." He fidgeted with his saddle again and then walked to the house. Uneasiness came over him suddenly. Once inside the kitchen, Joshua sat down. *"What Lord?"*

"Stay here."

"Why Lord? I always hear You better in the outdoors," whispered Joshua, somewhat confused. *"Besides, I need this time away and I've been looking forward to giving Dad a hand."*

The phone rang. Joshua let it ring a couple of times thinking his mom would pick up, but when it was on the third ring, he answered it.

"Hello."

"Joshua?"

"Yes."

"This is Mary, from the church office. I think Pastor Blair is having a heart attack. He is asking for you."

"Me? You better call an ambulance, Mary!"

"Joshua, can you come?"

"I'll be right there!"

Joshua put the phone back into its cradle as Belinda came into the kitchen.

"I wanted to make sure you had a sweater Joshua. It gets cold at nights," said Belinda, not looking at Joshua and trying to stuff the sweater into his saddlebag.

CHAPTER FIVE

"It's okay, Mom, I won't be going. Come on, we have to go to the church!"

"Why?"

"There's an emergency with Pastor Blair. Mary just called. She thinks he's having a heart attack!"

"Oh no, Joshua," gasped Belinda. "Did she call an ambulance?"

"I don't know."

On their way out to the truck, Joshua spotted a ranch hand and asked him to put his horse away.

Arriving at the church a few minutes later, Joshua and Belinda found Ken lying on a couch in his office. He was pale and perspiration glistened on his face, his breathing shallow.

"Mary, did you call an ambulance?"

Mary looked up at Joshua bending over Ken, her face stained with tears. "I called them right after I spoke with you. Pastor Blair asked me to call you first."

Joshua placed his hand on Ken's chest and began to petition the Lord on his behalf. *"Father, we lift Pastor Ken to You. Thank You for the stripes You took for his healing. We take authority over the spirit of fear. We thank You for Your healing power and . . ."*

WHEN TWO WORLDS COLLIDE

Loud knocking interrupted the prayer, and Mary jumped up to answer the door. Two paramedics rushed into the room. Joshua stepped aside to let them look at Ken.

"How long has he been in this state?" asked one of the paramedics, as he shone a light into Ken's eyes.

"He was getting chest pains about an hour ago. I wanted to call for an ambulance, but Pastor Blair told me to call Joshua," said Mary, her voice trembling.

The paramedic turned to Joshua. "Are you a doctor?"

"No."

"I'm afraid we can't do anything for him either."

Joshua looked at the paramedic not believing what he was hearing. "You mean he's dead?"

"If we had been called earlier, we might have been able to help him. We'll transport him to the hospital, but I'll need some information first."

"Can you give us a few moments with him?" asked Joshua.

The paramedics looked at each other. "Sure, we'll take our equipment to the ambulance and be back in a few minutes."

CHAPTER FIVE

After they left Joshua heard the Lord speaking to him, *"Keep your eyes fixed upon Me, Joshua. Do not look on the outward appearance. Do not doubt, only believe."*

Storing their equipment into the ambulance and calling in to report their findings, Terry and Ray stood by their vehicle looking at the church building. Terry took a cigarette from the package in his shirt pocket. He lit it and took a deep drag.

"Those things will kill you one day, buddy," commented Ray, as he watched Terry blow the smoke into the air.

Terry smiled. "Yeah, may be. Do you think the guy in there ever smoked? Sooner or later we all die; it's inevitable."

"I'd like to think my time is later. To answer your question, no this pastor never smoked. My wife and I use to go to his church."

"You go to church?" asked Terry surprised.

Ray laughed. "It's like this, I go to church Sunday morning and my wife comes with me Saturday night. It's a good trade off, don't you think?"

"I don't know, Ray, I wouldn't want any of that religious stuff rubbing off on me."

"I have such a hangover on Sunday, I never hear half of what they're saying anyway. It keeps my wife happy and it's only one day a week. I can handle it!"

Terry took another drag and flicked the butt to the ground, stepping on it. "We better get back in there and transport Pastor Blair to the hospital. They will need the death certificate signed by a doctor."

"Praise the Lord! Thank You Jesus!" shouted Mary and Belinda in unison, as Pastor Blair sat up.

Joshua continued to pray as color came back into Ken's face. Ken took a deep breath whispering, "Whew, what an experience, that was!"

"What did you see?" asked Joshua eagerly.

"It's not what I saw, Joshua, it's who I saw. I was at a river and Jesus was standing on the shore. He told me He was sending me back, as I still had work to do for Him. He . . . "

Terry and Ray came through the door at that moment, looking at Pastor Blair in total shock.

Ray spoke first. "We checked you thoroughly; you were dead."

Ken Blair smiled. "Well, as you can see, I'm very much alive. I was just telling these folks

CHAPTER FIVE

what happened to me." Ken didn't wait for approval, but dived right back into his story. "I was at a river and Jesus was there. He told me He was sending me back as I had more work to do for Him. He let me see Alice. She is so happy and content. My grief is so selfish. I have to let her go. We have so much to look forward to. Heaven is a glorious place!"

Terry needing more proof went back to the ambulance for the equipment. He poked and prodded until he was satisfied with the results. He then turned to Joshua. "What did you do to resuscitate him?"

"I prayed . . . we all prayed."

Terry and Ray packed up the equipment and looked for a quick escape.

"We're glad you're all right. We have to get back to the hospital," said Ray, as they walked to the door.

"Wait a minute," said Pastor Blair. "Do you know Jesus?"

Terry and Ray looked at each other and then to Ken. "Like we said, we have work to do," said Terry, "we don't have time to talk to you about religion."

Ken sighed heavily. "It's not about religion. It's about a relationship."

The two were already through the door with Ken's comment ringing in their ears.

WHEN TWO WORLDS COLLIDE

Speechless, Terry draped himself over the steering wheel and tried to make sense out of what just had happened. Ray began hearing his wife speak those same words to him. Even before he left for work this morning, his wife had prayed he would see she wasn't into religion, but had a relationship with Jesus Christ. He now felt awful for the way he had treated her and her belief. He looked at his watch. Just five more hours and he could talk to her about this experience. Terry started the truck not looking at Ray. He had many things to think about.

"Would you be interested in staying with us for awhile?" asked Belinda, pulling up a chair and sitting near Pastor Blair.
"Thank you Belinda, that's a good idea." Turning to Joshua he added, "I still need time away. After everything is in order here, I'll take you up on your offer of staying at the hunter's cabin."
"You're going up to the cabin, Pastor Blair?" asked Belinda, looking at Joshua puzzled with his statement.
"Yes. Joshua felt this would be a good place to get the rest and relaxation I need. Is this all right with you?"
"Certainly, I just didn't know anything about it."

CHAPTER FIVE

"I was going to fill you in Mom when I returned from helping Dad. If you're staying at the ranch Pastor Ken, I'll ride to camp and join Dad and Tyler."

"I'll be fine, Joshua. Thank you for your prayers."

"I haven't called Martin yet. He'll be wondering where his supper is," said Mary, as she patted Pastor Blair's hand. "I'll come round to Belinda's tomorrow and check up on you."

"No need, Mary, I'll be fine. Thank you for your support, but I need you here at the church. Could you phone the elders for me and have them come to the Coles'?"

"I'll phone them first thing in the morning. Pastor Blair, I'm so glad Jesus sent you back."

"Thank you, Mary. So am I."

CHAPTER SIX

The sun was setting when Joshua reached his dad's campsite. Weary from the ride, Joshua poured himself a cup of coffee and settled himself down in front of a blazing fire. After taking a couple of sips, Joshua looked up to see his dad and Tyler grinning from ear to ear.

"That sure was a wonderful thing the Lord did at the church, hey Joshua," beamed Tyler.

Joshua stared blankly at Tyler.

"You know," went on Tyler, "healing Pastor Blair the way He did!"

"What do you mean?"

Dan came over and sat down beside Joshua. "We saw what happened, Joshua."

"How could you, Dad? You were here checking on the cattle, remember?"

Dan nodded. "I remember just fine. Tyler and I received this persistent nudge from the Holy Spirit to stop what we were doing and pray for Pastor Blair. It was more than a nudge I guess; it was a burning sensation in both of us to get on our knees and pray. Now, this is going to be hard to believe, but both Tyler and I saw what was taking place with Pastor Blair. We took authority over the spirit of death and stood our ground for total healing for Pastor Blair's heart. As soon as you laid your hand on Pastor Blair, he was healed."

"You were here in the church when the paramedics diagnosed him, Dad? You knew he had died?"

"Yes. We had front row seats. We were here in full agreement as everyone prayed. We saw Jesus heal him. Jesus gave him a new heart and a new ministry. I believe our pastor will be evangelizing and praying for the sick."

"Did you see the same thing Dad saw, Tyler?"

"That's right Joshua. I knew in my head there was a spiritual world, but when we were actually there in the spirit, this world took on a whole new perspective. Our prayers definitely make a difference.

CHAPTER SIX

Praying in the Spirit or praying by the Spirit, takes you into realms where the Holy Spirit has full control. Now I know why satan takes such a whack at those who are filled with the Spirit. We can't walk this Spirit walk without being filled with Christ Jesus Himself."

"Tyler, how would you like to preach on Sunday?" asked Joshua, jokingly.

Tyler smiled. "You're called to be pastor and shepherd of the flock, Joshua. As you listen to the Holy Spirit, He will lead and guide you to the paths you are to walk on. Would you mind if I prayed for you?"

"Not at all."

Joshua stood while Dan and Tyler laid hands on him to pray.

"Father, we come to You in Jesus' name. We know You have called and prepared Joshua for ministry. Thank You for keeping a tight rein on his soul and causing him to walk on the straight and narrow path. Let Your Word have first place in his life. Let Your Word slice through all entanglements so he receives clear direction from You at all times. Father, thank You for the deep cleansing You are doing in his heart. Stir up those gifts You have placed within him, Father. Allow Joshua to see by his spiritual eyes so he does

not conform himself to this world's image."

Joshua groaned deeply and slumped to his knees. His body felt like lead, the weight of it forcing him to lie down. Then, suddenly he felt weightless. He could see himself lying on the ground, but he seemed to be above looking down. He sensed a hand on his shoulder and looked around. His heart raced. He stood looking into the face of Jesus, the very One who knew Joshua from the moment he was conceived to this moment in time.

"I will be with you Joshua, on the paths which you must walk. These journeys will not be easy, but know that I will be with you and I will never leave you alone. There are places you must go and the experiences will be hard, but I will be with you. Trust Me, Joshua. I will be with you. In a short while I will take you into a new country. My strength I give to you, My peace I leave with you. I love you Joshua."

Joshua slowly sat up feeling a little lightheaded. Dan helped him stand to his feet.

"So, what happened?" asked Tyler.

"I met Jesus. He said some things and then I woke up."

"What did He say, son?"

CHAPTER SIX

"I don't remember everything, Dad. The only thing that stuck with me is that I'm going to a new country."

"Is He sending you to Africa?" laughed Tyler.

"No, He didn't say anything about Africa. I'm sure He will show me when the time comes, though, what country He wants me in. Thanks for the prayer, I'll need all the help I can get come Sunday. I still haven't any idea what I'm suppose to say."

"Trust the Lord, Joshua," encouraged Dan, "He will give you the words to say."

"Yeah, that's another thing He said. I was to trust Him."

"I'm sure more will come back to you about what He said as He takes you on your journey."

"Dad, you didn't happen to be there when Jesus spoke to me, were you?"

"No."

"Well, you seem to be saying what He told me."

Dan smiled. "Well, if you're going to be in another country, we better get praying for your mother. She won't take this very well."

They all had a good chuckle together as they rolled out their sleeping bags. "See you

WHEN TWO WORLDS COLLIDE

in the morning, Josh," yawned Dan, as he pulled off his boots and crawled into his bed.

"Night, Dad. Night Tyler. This has been quite the day." Joshua pulled his blanket up to his chin and stared into the night sky. Stars winked at him through the blackened sky and the expanse of it all filled Joshua with awe. He had just stood face to face with the Creator of the universe and Joshua couldn't remember speaking a word.

Joshua stood at the podium of the little country church and scanned the faces. Some were shocked to see him instead of their regular pastor. Others looked indifferent. Others stifled a yawn or two and still others fussed with their little ones. What in the world was he suppose to say? He knew everyone was waiting. Dan and Belinda looked uncomfortable, but not as uncomfortable as he was. His heart raced and there wasn't a drop of saliva in his mouth. This wasn't how he imagined his first sermon to be. He was to be prepared with outline notes, scriptures to back up his statements, and a few jokes to break the ice. Nothing,

CHAPTER SIX

he had nothing. Joshua shifted to his other leg and continued to stare at the congregation. Now the people were getting restless. Someone cleared their throat and the sound echoed through the room. The pianist looked at Joshua, motioning to see if she could play something. Joshua shook his head. No, a song wasn't necessary, but what was? Just then a burning started in his chest and seeped up into his throat. The words were barely audible, slightly whispered. ***"Be still and know that I am God.[3]"***

The people looked at one another. Did he just say something, their expressions seemed to ask.

Joshua smiled. Yes, that was it! He spoke in an even voice this time, "Be still and know that I am God! Do we really know how to be still? The children are acting up and you tell them to be still. What are you expecting from them? Be still, be quiet, stop fiddling, shhhh. What is God expecting from us when He tells us to be still? I think He is saying to stop all activity. Stop and really listen, be still. Was that uncomfortable for you when all was silent? It was uncomfortable for me. After all, I'm standing up here and I'm supposed to say something. You were expecting me to say something. Well, God is saying something to you today, be still and know that He is God."

Joshua bowed his head. The sermon was over. The sermon was over? Is that all, Father, You want me to say? Okay. *"Father,"* prayed Joshua out loud, *"I bring these souls to You and ask You to teach us how to be still. I ask for Your protection for the rest of the week. I ask You to be with Pastor Blair as You strengthen him and give him the rest he needs. I ask these things in Christ's name, Amen."*

Joshua left the podium and walked to the back of the church. Not a single person moved or made any signs of leaving. Now what? The service was over and no one was leaving. Joshua found a seat in the back pew and sat down. He looked around. They all sat glued in their seats and no one spoke a word. Joshua felt a soft fluttering on his face and warmth permeating his chest. He couldn't move, didn't want to move and wondered if everyone else was having this experience too. He glanced over at his row. Yes, they were encountering God too. Silent tears flowed from one lady's face and the man next to her was

CHAPTER SIX

reaching for his hankie. God was here! Should he go back to the podium? No, he couldn't move. He bowed his head and spoke praises to God Almighty. What a wonderful time this was! Suddenly people stood on their feet and began shouting praises to God! Joshua joined them. "Thank You God! You are awesome and mighty, worthy to receive honor and praise! We love You!"

Some could barely speak as they left the church that day. The service turned out to be three hours long. The children were just as involved in the service as the adults were . . . a miracle, some said. No one congratulated Joshua on his sermon, everyone knew it wasn't Joshua; it was God who gave the sermon. People left excited and said they could hardly wait until next Sunday. As the church emptied, Joshua went back up to the pulpit and found his Bible. The only scripture spoken was, **'Be still and know that I am God.'** It was all they needed. Joshua shook his head. Bible school had not prepared him for this. He knew he would have lots to meditate on this coming week. And what about next Sunday? He would be just as excited, wondering what God was going to do. Is this what being still was all about? But what about preparing for a sermon, did God expect him to do that? Joshua closed his eyes and gripped the podium, a hand on either side. The words flowed over him like a soft gentle rain, *"Joshua, be still and know that I am God."*

Dan, Belinda and Pastor Blair sat at the dinner table waiting for Joshua to make his appearance. After splashing water on his face, Joshua looked in the mirror and grinned. What did God have in store for him? He almost trembled inside. Joshua left the bathroom and came to the table. "Looks good, Mom! I'm starving! Who's saying grace?"

Dan, Belinda, and Ken Blair looked at each other.

When no one answered, Joshua bowed his head and prayed, *"Father, thank You for the service this morning. We ask You to bless this food in Jesus' name, amen."* Joshua lifted his head and reached for the mashed potatoes. "Come on you guys, what's wrong? Aren't you hungry?"

"Joshua," started Belinda slowly, "what happened in the service this morning? Did you get the fluttering and warmth like a

CHAPTER SIX

blanket covering you? Did we really have God in our service this morning? Did you know He was coming? When did He give you the sermon?"

"Mom, you know as much as I do. He told me to speak out Psalm 46:10, which I did and He took it from there. I was just as shocked as you were. He didn't give me any indication of His plans. I'm quite looking forward to next Sunday. I wonder what He'll do then?"

"I wish I would have come this morning, Joshua," said Pastor Blair. "I think I'll wait and go fishing after next Sunday. I could use some revival in my own heart."

"Do you think this is what is happening, that a revival is coming?"

"Yes, Joshua. I think old Mrs. Smith's prayers are being answered. She was known to be as a looney tune, you know, not all there. But when she talked about heavenly places, her whole face lit up. You know, I think she really believed she had been to those places. She's been praying for revival for our valley for quite some time. I prayed with her a couple of times, but she gets some language that actually scared me. So I always came up with some kind of excuse so I didn't have to go pray with her.

WHEN TWO WORLDS COLLIDE

She was a faithful soul though; she would go pray even if she went by herself. People passing by said the lights were on way past midnight on Saturday nights."

"Where is she now?" asked Joshua, eager to meet this saint.

"Oh, she passed away last year. But as I recall, she did say God was sending a preacher to stir up the hearts of men. I knew she wasn't talking about me. Could be you Joshua." Pastor Ken put a couple of spoons of mashed potatoes on his plate and reached for the meat platter.

"I don't know," replied Joshua. "I'll have to see what God has planned. But one thing is for sure, I'm planning on being still and knowing that God is who He says He is."

After the ordination ceremony, Joshua was officially Pastor Joshua Cole. Pastor Ken could now take his leave of absence because a majority of the elders agreed to let Joshua fill in. He took a mobile phone and assured the Coles he would contact them when he was ready to come back.

CHAPTER SEVEN

"**M**rs. Pool, you have to have an appointment. You can't just go barging into the pastor's office," called Mary, hurrying after her.

Not knocking, Mrs. Pool swung the door open and stood towering over the pastor's desk. Joshua looked up from his reading and stared into Mrs. Pool's piercing eyes.

"I'm sorry, I . . . "

"It's okay Mary, I'll look after Mrs. Pool."

Mary turned to leave and shut the door behind her.

"Mary, could you please leave the door open?" Joshua asked.

Mary nodded and went back to her office.

"Now, Mrs. Pool, what's wrong?"

"Where's Pastor Blair?" demanded Mrs. Pool, almost shouting. "I'll not talk to some kid who's still wet behind the ears. I taught you in Sunday school, didn't I? No runny-nosed kid is going to run the church I attend!"

The pins, which kept her hair in place, loosened, and the stack of hair began tumbling down. Joshua tried not to laugh, but a snicker escaped.

"You find this funny?"

"You're hair, Mrs. Pool, it's . . ." began Joshua, but seeing the look on her face he decided not to finish his sentence.

Mrs. Pool fumbled around with her hair until it was no longer in her flushed face. Joshua took a deep breath. Why was she so riled up? For three Sundays in a row the power of God was so strong, people were healed and delivered. Where was Mrs. Pool all this time? Joshua had heard about her reputation, but seeing it firsthand was a little unnerving. He was about to say something when the Holy Spirit spoke into his heart, **"Be still."**

"Where did all the programs go? If you think I'm going to sit idle while you change everything, you've got another thing coming young man! We were doing just fine until you came along. I haven't been to service for three weeks because Mr. Pool had another stroke. There he sits in the

CHAPTER SEVEN

Applegate Nursing Home and not one person from this congregation has been to see him. I know he doesn't recognize anyone, but he gets lonely too." Mrs. Pool plopped herself down into a chair and said wearily, "I've had to keep up the farm and I'm tired. I can only see Mr. Pool on Sundays because the rest of the week I'm just too busy."

Joshua continued to pray as Mrs. Pool talked. His praying seemed to usher in the Presence of God.

Mrs. Pool took a breather and began to say something when she stopped and stared out the window. Suddenly she stood up. "You let me know when Pastor Blair gets back. I want to talk to him!"

Joshua didn't have a chance to reply. Mrs. Pool had already left. The air seemed suffocating, so Joshua left his office and found Mary, head bowed, at her desk.

Mary looked up. "I'm so sorry, Joshua. I tried to stop her, but she got past me. I couldn't believe all the things she was saying to you. I know Pastor Blair had his hands full with her monthly tirades at the board meetings. It was actually Conrad Pool who was the elder, but after he had the stroke, Ethel sat in for him. You sure handled the situation nicely."

"Mary, I couldn't speak. The Lord kept me quiet. I'm sure I could have said a number of things. If she was causing such a ruckus, I wonder why they let her stay? I guess it doesn't matter." Joshua paused for a moment before going on. "I was wondering if you could do some phoning for me. I'd like to change the meeting place for Sunday."

After he left the church, Joshua found solitude in his truck. *"You know Lord, I can't be cooped up in an office; I need wide open spaces. Thank You for ordering my steps today."*

A half-hour later, Joshua drove down the lane leading to the Pools' farm. Since Mr. Pool had been confined to a wheelchair, the place certainly needed some attention. Mrs. Pool was right; there was a lot of work to be done. Joshua noticed right off that the cattle's hay was quite a distance from where they were actually fed. He drove to the stack of hay and began loading the bales onto his truck. Now, this was where he felt at home. It felt good to do physical work again. After making a new stack where the feeding trough was, Joshua looked around for something else to do. The woodpile was dwindling, so

CHAPTER SEVEN

he found the axe and went to work. He was just finishing stacking the wood when Mrs. Pool drove in. She left her truck with her arms full of grocery bags. Joshua saw her struggling and hurried to her aid.

"Here, let me give you a hand."

Mrs. Pool eyed him suspiciously and gave up one bag. "What are you doing here? I don't need any charity from you, young man!"

"It's not charity, Mrs. Pool. We're here on this earth to serve one another. I'm here to serve you today."

"Is that a fact?"

Joshua stood in the kitchen at the back door and handed Mrs. Pool his bag.

"Take your boots off. I've got a plugged kitchen sink you can fix!"

Joshua obeyed. Mrs. Pool handed him a plunger and went to work unpacking her groceries. The plunger didn't seem to work. Joshua went out to his truck and retrieved his tools. After taking the pipe apart and cleaning the drainpipe, the water flowed down the sink unhindered. He made sure everything under the sink was put back in order. Before he made his way to his truck, he said goodbye to Mrs. Pool. Joshua sat in the truck a few minutes before starting it up. Mrs. Pool certainly was a crusty old lady. Bowing his head, Joshua prayed, *"Father, please show me Your plan for Mrs. Pool. What I do here for her, I do as unto You. May she see You in me and help me to walk in Your love."*

Joshua's next stop was the Applegate Nursing Home. He spoke with the administrator so everything was set for Sunday. He then went to Mr. Pool's room. Mr. Pool sat in his wheelchair staring blankly. He drooled from his open mouth. Joshua's heart began to ache. He remembered a time when no one dared stand in Mr. Pool's way. He used to stand six feet, with broad shoulders, and muscles rippling from his tanned arms. Now he wasn't the same man. His thin frame sagged in the chair and his arms hung limply from his shoulders. Joshua stood in front of him and extended his hand. Mr. Pool did not move. Joshua reached for his hand and gripped it in his.

"Hello, Mr. Pool." Joshua held his hand for a moment and placed it back into Mr. Pool's lap. Joshua pulled a chair up beside him. "You probably don't remember me, but I'm Joshua Cole. I haven't been around here for a few years because I've been in Bible school. They call me Pastor

CHAPTER SEVEN

Joshua now. Hard to believe isn't it? You know all the trouble Hank and I use to get into. What is Hank doing anyway? They say he joined the navy and is stationed in Hawaii. I'll have to ask Mrs. Pool if she's heard from him lately. Well, I have a few more stops to make before getting home to my own chores. It was nice chatting with you. I'll see you on Sunday."

Mr. Pool's expression had not changed through the whole conversation, but Joshua felt that he had heard him. Joshua gripped Mr. Pool's hand again and left the room. Walking down the hallway, Joshua looked at other faces staring blankly ahead. *Oh Father, how do we get so trapped in these bodies? Your Word is health and healing to all our flesh. How do Your Words transfer from the page to our bodies? Show me Father, how to pray and see Your healing power.*

Joshua made one last stop at the Lindens before going home. Madison wasn't home so he gave the information to Joan. He wanted to make sure the Lindens

WHEN TWO WORLDS COLLIDE

would be at the Applegate Nursing Home on Sunday morning. Madison needed to see how blessed she really was, even if she was in a wheelchair. Joan thanked Joshua and said they would be there.

Belinda stood at the sink peeling potatoes when Joshua came in.

"Hi! How was your day, Josh?"

"Interesting."

Belinda wiped her hands on a towel and faced Joshua. "Why do you say that?"

"I had a run-in with Mrs. Pool. She sure had her dander up. Guess she's worried about Mr. Pool. He's had another stroke."

"I'm sorry to hear that. Mrs. Pool though, is one woman I stay away from. She can get me so riled; she seems to know every button to push in me. I don't think she has many friends either."

"Do you think she's born-again, Mom?"

"I think she did give her heart to the Lord a couple of summers ago when we had that evangelist come through. Both of the Pools went forward at the camp meeting."

"Well, that's good news," said Joshua sounding relieved. "I guess the Lord has something planned then for Sunday."

"Meaning?"

"The Lord told me to have the service at

CHAPTER SEVEN

the Applegate Nursing Home. Mary is busy calling everyone. I've talked with the administrator and we can use the dining room Sunday morning. We looked at the chapel, but it was too small. He seemed quite excited about it."

"You can't do that Joshua. We have church in a church, not in some nursing home!"

Joshua's smile disappeared. "What are you saying, Mom?"

"I wouldn't feel comfortable worshipping in a nursing home." Belinda looked perplexed. "I'm also disturbed with what's been happening for the last few weeks. It's just not the same any more. Pastor Blair had a program; everyone knew what was going on. Now there doesn't seem to be any structure. I don't know if I like this change."

Joshua couldn't believe what he was hearing. Did everyone in the fellowship feel like this? Actually, these were some of the same things Mrs. Pool had voiced today. This move of the Holy Spirit was new to him too. He learned one method in school and the Lord was changing his whole perspective. It seemed Sunday after Sunday, he was only able to quote one or two scriptures, and then the Holy Spirit took over. Joshua would not quench the Holy Spirit.

"I suggest then, Mom, you talk to the Lord about what you're feeling. I'm only doing what He says, and frankly, it isn't much. I haven't even given a sermon yet. And about the church meeting place, it's not about a building. We are the church and the kingdom of God is within us, right?"

"I don't know what to think anymore, Joshua. I just wish Pastor Blair were here so I could talk to him. He has the mobile phone and he said he would call when he was ready to come back. He's been up there for two weeks; you'd think that was long enough to sort things out. I hope he's all right."

"So, you think things would be better if Pastor Ken were here?"

Belinda looked at Joshua and then back to her unpeeled potatoes. Facing Joshua again, she said, "I just knew I could count on Pastor Blair. It was structured, Josh. I miss that. This new thing is scaring me; it's just so explosive! One minute we're singing, the next it's total silence, or someone has fallen from his or her seat. Something is happening to me; I'm not sure how to put it into words."

"I'm sorry I disappoint you, but I won't quench the Holy Spirit. He said to have the

CHAPTER SEVEN

meeting at the nursing home, so that's where we'll be Sunday morning. I know I haven't had years of experience like Pastor Ken, he . . . Joshua stopped and listened . . . ***Be still . . .***"

"What," persisted Belinda, "finish what you were going to say?"

Joshua just stared at his mother and then put on his jacket. "I'll be back after chores."

Belinda looked down at the potatoes and then at the ceiling. *"What are You doing to me? Why won't Joshua listen? I don't want to see him get hurt. I just want a little structure. I need to know what's going on!"*

"Who are you talking to, Belinda?" asked a voice in her ear.

Startled, Belinda jumped and cut her finger on the peeler. "Dan Cole, look what you made me do!"

"Here, let me look at that. Awe, its just a little nick. You'll live," laughed Dan, rubbing Belinda's back and pulling her close.

Belinda tried to pull away, but Dan held on. Belinda relaxed and let Dan hold her.

"I'm worried about Joshua."

"Why? He's a big boy, he can look after himself. Come on, let's go talk about it."

Belinda shook her head. "I've got to start supper . . ."

"Supper can wait." Dan backed away from Belinda and took her hand in his as he pulled her through the hallway to the family room. He sat down on the couch and Belinda eased in beside him. "Okay, what's really wrong?"

Belinda sighed heavily. "I'm scared, Dan. Nothing is the same; everything is changing. I want Pastor Blair to come back. I don't like what is happening with our church. You can never count on anything being the same. It's getting too emotional."

Dan thought for a moment. "So, what you're saying then, is that you don't want God to be in control? You want man to be in control?"

"That's not what I mean, Dan. God has given us pastors and teachers, so why isn't Joshua being a pastor? He said himself; he hasn't even given a sermon yet. And Joshua is spending way too much time with Madison Linden. She's only seventeen, for heaven's sake!"

"Whoa, now where is this coming from? You went from talking about the fellowship to Madison in one breath. What is really happening in you, Belinda? I think you have to let go of Joshua. I think this is the root of your problem. You can't control

CHAPTER SEVEN

Joshua and you certainly can't control what is happening in the church."

Belinda folded her arms defiantly. "I'm just trying to be a good mother!"

"No, you're trying to control and manipulate Joshua. Listen, Belinda, our parenting days are over; we have to let Joshua make his own way now. He'll make good decisions and bad ones, but the Lord has promised to be with him in all his ways. You're a good mother," whispered Dan as he snuggled closer to Belinda. "I'll finish peeling the potatoes and we'll go for a ride after supper. We'll ride up to the ridge and watch the sunset."

In years past, Belinda's stubbornness wouldn't have allowed her to back down so easily, but she decided to listen to Dan. She didn't want Joshua to leave her, and she would keep a close eye on Madison Linden.

CHAPTER EIGHT

The Applegate Nursing Home was filled to capacity; people were even standing in the hallway. Joshua felt excitement, but also nervousness. He didn't have anything planned. All he heard over the past week was to be still. One thing he knew for sure. These people weren't coming to see him; they were coming to see God. Some of his mother's words tried to penetrate his mind, but Joshua came against the negative thoughts. Joshua stood up and bowed his head, "Father, we desire to lift up Your name today. We've come here to worship You. You know every person in this building and what their heart's cry is. I know You can meet all of their needs. We invite You, Holy Spirit, to take control of this meeting. We give this service to You." Joshua sat down.

WHEN TWO WORLDS COLLIDE

It started quietly, an angelic voice penetrating the atmosphere, but as the voice gained more confidence, it grew stronger and stronger. The words were clear and distinct, but not a tongue anyone understood. It soothed and rocked the tattered soul. People began weeping softly. Then the voice stopped, but began once again in the same melody, in a tongue this time, everyone could understand, *"My children, I love you. Come to Me, all you who are weary and heavy-laden, and I will give you rest. You can rest in Me. I will never leave you. I Am here for you."*

Everyone was awed by His Presence. Mrs. Pool took her husband's hand and found strength in his grip. She looked over and he smiled back. He put his hands on the sides of his chair and slowly stood up. Everyone around him began clapping and shouting praises to God. Joshua quickly left his seat and stood beside Mr. Pool as he swayed slightly. Mr. Pool could feel the power of God flowing through his body. He was free, no longer trapped by the after effects of the stroke. Ethel Pool began sobbing, "Thanks be to God! He is our healer! Forgive us of our unbelief, oh forgive us, God!"

People began falling to their knees in repentance. Others cried out for forgiveness

CHAPTER EIGHT

and many others shouted praises into the heavenlies. The service which was to last an hour and a half was coming to a close three hours later. The staff wanted to set up for lunch, but couldn't get into the dining room. Joshua sensed their tension.

"If anyone wants further prayer," announced Joshua, "we'll go back to the church. We must let the staff in here to set up for lunch."

It was hard to leave, but people began making their way to the parking lot. Mr. Pool decided he didn't want lunch. Instead, he left with Mrs. Pool. It was truly a miracle to see them walk hand in hand out of the nursing home.

Nobody wanted to go home as they thought if the Lord were to manifest His presence again, they didn't want to miss it. Joshua looked around and saw new faces. Excitement filled the air. Not even the pull of lunchtime could sway these people to leave. Joshua glanced down at his watch. It was after four. The Lindens were near the back of the church so Joshua approached them.

WHEN TWO WORLDS COLLIDE

"Do you need prayer?" asked Joshua, directing the question to Madison.

Madison nodded. "I asked Jesus into my heart when I was little, but now I want to make Him Lord." Madison shifted in her chair and continued, "I want to surrender everything to Jesus."

Both parents knelt down as Joshua prayed. *"Father, we lift Madison to You. You see her hearts' desire and we thank You for answering her."*

Madison lifted up her head and smiled. "I know what happened today can only come from God. I've never had a song of the Lord before, but after singing it out, I want to do everything He desires of me."

Shocked Joshua asked, "Really, Madison, that was you? The song was beautiful."

Madison looked at Joshua shyly, "I knew God had given me a singing voice, but I was always too scared to sing. I'm surrendering my voice to Him today too."

Joan and Edward Linden hugged their daughter and audibly gave thanks for a daughter who had been renewed.

"Please come over and have supper with us, Joshua," offered Joan.

"Sure, that would be great. Let me give my mom a call and I'll meet you at your place."

CHAPTER EIGHT

Joshua went to the office and dialed the number.

"Mom?"

"Where are you Joshua? I've been holding dinner for over an hour."

"Just letting you know I'm going over the Linden's."

"Why?"

Joshua hesitated. "Um, because they asked me."

There was a long pause and Joshua heard his mom sigh deeply.

"Fine, we'll go ahead without you then."

"Okay, see you later." Joshua put the phone back into its cradle. Why was his mom acting so strange? They had all just experienced a powerful move of the Holy Spirit. Shouldn't she be excited? He would have a word with her when he got home. *Thank You Father, for Madison's new commitment. Help me to disciple her in all Your ways."*

Joshua pushed himself away from the table. "Joan, that was excellent."

"Would you like another piece of pie?"

WHEN TWO WORLDS COLLIDE

Joshua groaned. "No thank you, two pieces is my limit. Well, actually one piece would have been enough, but it was so good."

Joan smiled and began cleaning off the table. Joshua stood and started to help her. "Please Joshua, I'll do this. You and Madison go out on the porch and I'll bring you some coffee. Edward is finishing up with the chores and will join you later."

Madison was already wheeling herself to the door when Joshua caught up to her. He opened the door for her and Madison wheeled through it. Joshua pulled up a chair and sat beside her.

"So, how are you feeling, Madison?" asked Joshua, gazing into her bright blue eyes.

"Full."

"No, I mean about rededicating your life to Jesus."

"Fine, but I was expecting more I guess. After seeing Mr. Pool's miracle, I . . ."

"Were you expecting to be healed too?"

Madison lowered her eyes and nodded.

Joshua took her hand and squeezed it. "I'll agree with you for your complete healing, Madison. I'm not sure why it didn't

CHAPTER EIGHT

happen all at once, but waiting on the Lord is a wonderful experience."

Madison looked up at Joshua. She was sure her heart skipped a beat when he took her hand in his. Just being this close to him also affected her breathing. He was so handsome. His eyes were brown, but had flecks of gold in them. His collar length hair was sandy blond and a few wisps fell on his forehead. Madison thought him to be about six feet tall, but then it was hard to tell from a wheelchair. If she could stand, she could fit easily under the crook of his arm and . . .

"Did you hear me, Madison?"

"Sorry, what did you say?"

"Did you want to go riding tomorrow?"

"Sure. Can we use Brandy again?"

"You're beginning to like her, aren't you? She's a good mount for you. Mom won't mind."

"I do like Brandy. Please let your mom know I really appreciate her letting me use her horse. Dad said he would get me another horse some day."

"Would you consider attending the new Christians class at the church? Have you ever attended a class like that before?"

"No, I've never attended one. Will you be teaching it?"

WHEN TWO WORLDS COLLIDE

"Yes, I'll be teaching the class, Madison. I think Mr. and Mrs. Pool will be there too. I'll be letting others know it will be available." Joshua sipped his coffee and wondered again about his mom's reaction on the phone. He looked over at Madison. She was very pretty. Her long blond hair lay softly around her shoulders. Was it as silky as it looked? It was tempting to take a few strands in his fingers to see. Joshua almost shook his head. What was he thinking? She was a friend, nothing more. Joshua stood up. "I best be getting home. I'll say goodbye to your mom and set up a time with her for our riding."

"Sure, P.J. I'll be looking forward to our riding." Madison smiled up at him.

"By the way, Madison, I've had some negative feedback on what you call me. May be we could just stick to Joshua or Pastor Cole."

"All right," said Madison puzzled. "It's just that we both agreed."

"I know Madison, sorry. I guess I didn't think on how it would sound to other people."

"Like it's too personal, Pastor Cole?"

"Yeah, I guess so. But then Pastor Cole sounds too formal for friends. Just call me Joshua."

CHAPTER EIGHT

"Okay Joshua, see you tomorrow."

Joshua took his coffee cup and went inside the house. After he spoke to Joan and set up a time with her, he strode toward his truck. Once inside he turned and waved at Madison before driving off.

Joan came out and joined Madison on the porch.

Mom, do pastors ever marry?"

Joan laughed. "He's not a priest, Madison and yes, pastors do marry. Why do you ask?"

"I'm going to marry Joshua Cole!"

"Don't get your hopes up, Madison. I think he's too old for you. Besides, I'm sure his mother will have something to say about whom he marries. Madison, we don't fit into their circle, they're very wealthy."

Madison listened to what her mom was saying but didn't agree. "Joshua isn't like that, Mom, and besides, he makes his own decisions. Has Mrs. Cole said something?"

"No, dear. It's not in what she says, but the way she acts around Joshua. She keeps a close eye on him. It's nice to have dreams, Madison, but I don't think you should include Pastor Joshua Cole into them."

"What's this about marriage?" asked Edward Linden, taking a seat beside his wife.

WHEN TWO WORLDS COLLIDE

Joan ignored the question and took her husbands' arm. "What a wonderful decision Madison has made for the Lord. What Bible studies we can have together now!"

Edward glanced at both his wife and daughter and knew he wasn't going to get an answer. "Our prayers have been answered, Madison." He patted Madison's hand and smiled.

Madison added, "Joshua wants me to attend a new Christians class he is teaching. He'll let us know the day and time."

Edward and Joan smiled at their daughter. This was a good day!

Joshua didn't go right home. He stopped in to see the Pools first. Mrs. Pool was in the yard when Joshua drove in. She was grinning.

"Joshua, I didn't know what to think when you changed the church service to the nursing home. I wondered what you were up to," commented Mrs. Pool, as she walked with Joshua to the house.

Once inside, Joshua sat on a chair and the Pools sat on a couch across the room from him.

"Can I get you anything, Joshua?" asked Mrs. Pool.

CHAPTER EIGHT

"No thanks. I just finished a meal with the Lindens."

"Did the Lord tell you to have the service at the nursing home?" asked Mrs. Pool eagerly. "You know, I wasn't going to go this morning. I was quite upset with you, but I'm glad I went. I've been so tired looking after everything and when the Lord touches other people and nothing is happening in your own life, it's just so unfair."

"You know Ethel, I've been feeling the same way," added Mr. Pool. "Joshua stopped in here the other day and I just knew something was going to happen." Conrad Pool paused for a moment and continued. "I could hear everything people were saying, I just couldn't respond. It was so darn frustrating."

"Joshua went to see you?"

Joshua felt he was in on a private conversation so he continued to keep still.

"He sure did Ethel. He talked to me like I could hear and understand . . . made me feel like a man again. Some people treat you like you're brain dead or something. Used to make me real ornery inside and if I could have responded, I would have given them an earful." Conrad laughed. "Guess it was best I couldn't talk."

Ethel laughed too. It was amazing how many years seemed to fall off her face as she laughed. Laughter was truly good medicine for the soul.

"Joshua, I mean Pastor Cole," started Ethel, "would you forgive me for being so bullheaded the other day?"

"Yes, Mrs. Pool, and please call me Joshua."

"If you'll call me Ethel."

"Now, that's going to be rather difficult," said Joshua, "I've known you all my life as Mr. and Mrs. Pool, but I'll try."

"I won't be attending the elder's meetings, Joshua. Until Conrad gets his strength back, I'll be sticking close to home. I want to spend every moment with him, because time is so short," said Ethel, taking his hand in hers.

Joshua thought about how relieved the elders would be when he told them of Ethel's decision. "Whatever you think is best, Ethel. And Conrad, try not to do too much too quickly, allow the Lord to continue to give you strength."

"You know, I sensed the Lord saying that to me too, Joshua. Since His healing power flowed through my body, I can hear His voice much clearer now. My doctor phoned and wants to see me tomorrow.

CHAPTER EIGHT

It'll be interesting to see what he'll find." Conrad paused and continued, "I was wondering if you could give Ethel and I a hand until I get back on my feet. I mean to pay you, of course. Ethel will fix up the bunkhouse. What do you think?"

Joshua smiled. "I'll do whatever I can to help you. Dad probably won't need me; he has enough hands right now. I do have some responsibilities at the church, so they come first."

"Fine, Joshua, fine. We'll get things in order and see you in a couple of days," said Conrad, as he stood to shake Joshua's hand in agreement. Ethel and Conrad stood in the doorway and watched Joshua leave.

"You're changing, Conrad," cooed Ethel, snuggling up to him. "You never let anyone help you before."

"I know Ethel, and I wasn't about to this time, but I felt the Lord telling me to. For some reason, this is going to help Joshua too." Conrad tried to stifle a yawn. "I'm rather tired. Think I've had enough excitement for one day."

"I've a couple of things left to do outside, but will be in to join you soon." Ethel put her arms around her husband. "It's nice to have you home!"

CHAPTER NINE

"Morning, Mom," yawned Joshua, as he poured himself a cup of coffee.

Belinda looked up from her reading. "Where were you yesterday? Even though you didn't show up for dinner, I waited up for you until quite late. Dad and I have a few things to discuss with you and you were nowhere to be found," accused Belinda, glaring at Joshua.

"Hold on, Mom, what's wrong?"

"What do you mean?"

"I have responsibilities and I don't need to answer to you about where I was. What's this really about?"

"Joshua Cole, you're living under our roof and we do have some say! I want to know what your intentions are for Madison Linden. Remember she is only seventeen and you're twenty-two. And if . . ."

WHEN TWO WORLDS COLLIDE

Joshua stood up angrily. "Mother, I don't know what your problem is, but you've said enough. I'm moving to the Pools. I'll talk to you later, once we've both cooled down!"

"What do you mean you're moving to the Pools?" Belinda followed Joshua into his bedroom and watched as he retrieved his suitcases from the closet. "I can't believe you would move in with those people." Belinda felt a check in her spirit to be quiet, but ignored it and pressed on. "You can't use your title to pursue this girl, and that's what Madison Linden is . . . a little girl!"

"Please be quiet, Mother!" Joshua put his hands on her shoulders and turned her around facing the door. "Please get out of my room."

After Belinda left, Joshua sat wearily on the side of the bed. What was going on? He knew his mom to be a bit of a controller, but this was ridiculous. What did Madison have to do with all of this? He would have to set up riding at the Pools and begin looking for another horse for Madison. He wouldn't ask to use Brandy now. As he finished packing his heart burned. Why was his mom so angry? May be his dad had some answers. He would look for him when he had everything packed in his truck.

CHAPTER NINE

Joshua found his dad unloading sacks of grain. "Hi Josh, did you sleep in?"

"A little. Mom and I just had a huge fight. Do you know what's wrong with her?"

Dan threw the next sack down on the pile and looked at Joshua. "Her little boy has grown up and she doesn't want to let him go. When Roberta Cleveland called, it turned her world upside down."

"And what about my world, Dad? The Lord gave me you both as my parents; it was no accident. I struggled too with this revelation, but I know it's best to leave it in the Lord's hands."

"You and I both know that, but your mom refuses to see. I know she needs to allow the Holy Spirit to heal her inner self. She's very strong willed."

"In the letter Roberta gave me, it seems the Shrivers in Cochrane . . . would like to meet me. They said they wouldn't press the issue, but leave the decision with me. I didn't tell you before because I didn't want to upset you. I've been in touch with them and I'll go to Canada one day to meet them."

"I figured you would choose to meet them, Joshua, but I don't think your mom is ready to hear this. Can we keep it between us?"

"I guess so. I came to tell you I'm moving

to the Pools. I'd like to help Conrad until he gets his strength back."

"You're a good man, Joshua. I'm proud to know you." Dan hugged his son.

"When I'm finished at the Pool's, I won't be coming back here. I need my own place, Dad."

"I know Josh, I know. Would you consider moving into the log house your mom and I use to live in?"

Joshua shook his head. "No thanks, Dad. I'm thinking of buying the piece of land by the Lindens. Could you come and take a look at it with me? I'd like to know what you think."

"You bet. Can I finish unloading the grain first?"

"Sure, I'll give you a hand."

Dan surveyed the land and nodded in approval. "This is a fine piece of property, Joshua. There's good water and the buildings are well-situated. Will you put an offer on it?"

"Yes." Changing the subject, Joshua asked, "Do you think Mom would sell Brandy?"

CHAPTER NINE

"I don't know. Still rides her once in awhile; do you have a rider in mind?"

"Madison Linden."

Dan smiled. "I see. So her riding is improving, then?"

"She's doing really well. You should see her in the saddle; you'd never know she came out of a wheelchair. And don't look at me like that; she's just a friend. Did you know she rededicated her life to Christ yesterday?"

"No, but I'll bet her mom and dad were excited."

"They were. Madison will be going to the new Christians class along with Ethel and Conrad."

"You're mom will be happy to have some new people in her class. Did you know Pastor Blair put her in charge of the class?"

"No. I was going to teach it, but if Pastor Ken has asked Mom to take it, I'll have to talk to her. By the way, have you heard from Pastor Blair?"

"Yes, your mom talked to him yesterday. I guess he'll be back next week. I don't know about him coming back to his duties at the church, but she's picking him up. By the way she was talking, I think she's the one who contacted him. Personally, I

WHEN TWO WORLDS COLLIDE

don't think he's ready to come back. I don't know what your mom is up to, but I'm praying."

"I wonder why Mom didn't mention it to me?"

"I'm not sure son, may be it slipped her mind. You're close with your mom Josh; this situation is just a little bump in the road. Things will be all right."

Joshua nodded still troubled about his confrontation with his mom. Joshua went to town after leaving his dad, to find the Real Estate office that had listed the property. After finding the office and speaking to the realtor, he put in his offer and waited. Several hours later, because the owner was looking for a quick settlement, Joshua was the new owner. He could hardly wait to share his good news!

"Well, that's wonderful Joshua!" exclaimed Ethel Pool.

"I'm still available to help you. I just won't be living here," said Joshua. "What can I do today?"

Just then Conrad came into the

CHAPTER NINE

kitchen. He walked over to Ethel and kissed her lightly on the cheek. "Please, Conrad, we have company!"

"Aw, I'm sure Joshua has seen couples kiss before," laughed Conrad. "This is such a wonderful day! Praise God for His faithfulness!"

Joshua grinned. Most of the hard lines on Ethel's face were fading and Conrad had a new twinkle in his eye. The miraculous had invaded the physical world, showing itself in healing to the body and soul of Ethel and Conrad Pool. Joshua hoped they might soon give their testimony at church.

CHAPTER TEN

Joshua looked up at Pastor Ken Blair standing behind the pulpit and sighed heavily. The Presence of God, which each Sunday was so prevalent, now seemed to be on vacation. Everything changed when Pastor Blair came back. The once filled building had many empty pews. It was business as usual. Joshua longed for the Presence of the Holy Spirit to envelope them once again.

Pastor Blair sat down and Belinda Cole came to the podium. "Please turn to hymn number 307, 'Jesus Lover Of My Soul.'" The rustle of paper could be heard, but Joshua didn't turn there. If he had to endure one more gleeful look from his mother, he would be sick. Joshua stood up and left the church. To his surprise, people followed him.

WHEN TWO WORLDS COLLIDE

"I'm sorry Pastor Cole, but I couldn't take another minute of that service. We want God, not some program. Can you help us find a place to worship?" petitioned a man from one of the families.

"Let's go back in there and tell Pastor Blair our desire."

"I've tried to talk to him," added another man. "Seems the Coles are running the show these days. Sorry, Pastor Cole, not you, but your mother. She's got Pastor Blair all riled up against us."

Oh Mother, what have you done? What this man was saying was so true, but going back in there would just cause more factions. He felt a peace cover him then and said, "Okay, let's go to my place and wait upon the Lord."

Each face seemed to light up as they hurried to their vehicles. Joshua didn't see the Lindens in church this morning. He would be going there later for Madison's birthday supper. He could hardly wait to give her the present he bought. She was going to be so surprised!

"Where two or three are gathered together in My name, I am there in the midst of them,[4]" quoted Joshua.

Everyone crowding into Joshua's living

[4] Matthew 18:20

CHAPTER TEN

room listened intently and pondered the scripture Joshua spoke.

"Please share what God has done for you," suggested Joshua.

A man stood and said, "I was having a real problem with nicotine. I knew I should quit, but this thing had a real hold on me. I decided to give it to Jesus and ask Him for His help. I haven't had a cigarette or a chew in two weeks."

Everyone clapped and spoke out words of encouragement. The next person to stand was a young boy. "It's been hard to come to church because my mom and dad wouldn't bring me. So I put them on God's altar and left them with Him." The boy looked down at his parents seated nearby, whose eyes were welling with tears. "Guess God must've wanted them."

Everyone began sharing what was on their hearts. Petitions and praise poured forth as they waited on the Lord. God was definitely here. Before the meeting closed, everyone wanted to know if they could meet at Joshua's next week. Joshua agreed. He knew he would have to talk to Pastor Blair. Why hadn't Pastor Blair come back refreshed? Joshua actually knew the answer to his own question. His mother.

WHEN TWO WORLDS COLLIDE

When would she leave well enough alone and let the Lord be in control? Thinking about it gave him an immediate headache, so Joshua tried to clear his mind. Remembering what the young boy had earlier shared, Joshua prayed, *"I give my mom to You, Lord she belongs to You."*

After Joshua loaded his present for Madison, he drove over to their place. He parked over by the barn so he could retrieve his surprise later. It seemed quiet and Joshua wondered where the rest of the guests were. He knocked on the front door. Looking at his watch, it was nearly five. He was right on time. Joshua heard voices and then Joan came to the door. Her face beamed, "Sorry, I didn't hear you knocking Joshua. Come in!"

"Did I get the time wrong?"

"No, you're right on time. I'll get Madison and Edward."

Joshua sat down in the living room and waited. Excited voices filled the hallway, and when Joshua saw Madison, he jumped up. Madison walked over to him wearing a frilly dress. "Maddie, you're walking! When? How?" questioned Joshua, stammering.

CHAPTER TEN

"Early this morning my back began to burn, then it felt like someone was pouring water over me. I put my legs over the side of the bed and stood up. It was awesome, Joshua! I've been healed!"

Then Joan bubbled over, "I went into Madison's room and when I didn't find her in bed, I really got scared. My calling woke up Edward, and both of us went to look for her. We found her skipping through the pasture. What a wonder to behold! We rubbed our eyes . . . yes, our Madison was healed!"

Joshua thought his heart would burst as he hugged Madison. What a wonderful birthday present from God.

Madison put her arms around Joshua and clung to him. All of her dreams were coming true!

Joshua took Madison's hand and walked with her to the barn. He left her standing near his trailer, as he unloaded his present.

Madison gasped, "Oh, he's beautiful, Joshua." He was dark brown and had three white stockings. He had a perfect diamond shaped star on his forehead. Madison took the lead rope from Joshua and led him into the corral.

"What's his name?"

"His registered name is, 'He's a Blazen', but you can call him whatever you want."

"Thank you so much, Joshua, he's wonderful! I'll call him Blaze. What do you think?"

"This is quite an extravagant gift, Joshua," commented Edward, stroking the horse. "He's a thoroughbred, isn't he?"

"Well, actually, a quarter horse crossed with a thoroughbred. I should've consulted with you first, but when I saw him, I just knew this was the horse for Maddie! He's spirited, but I know she can handle him, I've seen the way she rides."

"Does your mom and dad know you've purchased this horse for Madison?" asked Joan concerned.

"No." Changing the subject, Joshua added, "I just purchased the place across the road from you. I'm not living with Mom and Dad."

"Really, Josh," exclaimed Madison. "We wondered who the new owners were."

"It's a nice piece of property," said Edward approvingly. "I'm glad we'll be neighbors."

Joshua locked eyes with Madison. "I'm glad too, Edward."

CHAPTER TEN

"Let's go for a ride, Joshua! You can use dad's horse!"

"Hold on, Madison," said Joan, "your birthday supper is just about ready and we're still expecting some more guests." Joan looked at Joshua. "I hope you don't mind Joshua. I've invited your mom and dad."

"If Mother behaves it will be fine. She's been acting pretty weird lately."

They left Blaze munching some hay in the corral and went back up to the house. Walking along side Joshua, Joan continued her conversation. "I know, Joshua, I've seen it too. I thought if she got to know us better she would see we aren't a threat to her, though . . .I've seen the way you look at Madison."

Joshua smiled. "I know, it caught me by surprise today, Joan. I would like to date your daughter."

Madison caught up to them. "What are you two talking about?"

Joshua casually put his arm around Madison's waist as they neared the house. "I was asking permission to date you, Madison."

"To date me, actually go somewhere as a couple, Joshua?"

Joshua laughed. "Yeah, something like that."

Madison then looked at her mom and dad for approval. "We respect you, Joshua," agreed Edward, "and we know you'll look after our girl."

Madison looked up at Joshua and then kissed him lightly on the cheek. "Thank you for the birthday present; he's awesome! We'll go for a ride later, okay?"

"It's a date Maddie."

Madison smiled and followed her mom into the house. Inside Madison hugged her mom. "Didn't I tell you mom, one day I will be Mrs. Madison Cole."

"He's dating you Madison, not marrying you."

"You'll see, Mom. I predict sometime soon, I'll be married to Joshua Cole."

"Well, for now we need to get this table set. The Coles should be here any minute."

The dinner seemed to go well and because Madison was seated when the Coles arrived, Belinda and Dan didn't know of the miracle across the table from them. When the cake, with all of the candles, was placed in front of Madison, she stood to blow them out.

"Madison, you're standing!" exclaimed Dan. "When did this happen?"

CHAPTER TEN

"I was healed early this morning."

Belinda looked at Joshua and how he was looking at Madison. Was that a look of love she saw? Wait until she got him alone, he would have some explaining to do. She promised Dan she wouldn't start anything, so for now she would be still. She glanced up at Madison. If that little girl, for one moment, thought she was going to steal her son away from her, she had another thing coming.

"Belinda, Belinda," prodded Dan, "isn't it wonderful about Madison's healing?"

Every eye was on Belinda. She could feel it and struggled with something nice to respond with. "The Lord is good, and now you will have something to share with the class tomorrow night."

"I won't be coming back to the class, Mrs. Cole."

"What do you mean?"

"I'll talk to you later, Mrs. Cole. I don't want to talk about it here."

"But you've already brought it up dear, so go ahead, what's your problem?"

"I won't be the brunt of your snide remarks any longer, Mrs. Cole. All you talk about is how I'm no good for Joshua."

"Mother, is this true?"

WHEN TWO WORLDS COLLIDE

"It's not all the time. She's exaggerating. I want to know her intentions since you never talk to me any more," replied Belinda pouting.

Dan looked at Belinda. "You're unbelievable." He stood up, "I'm sorry, but we have to go. Thanks for your hospitality and the dinner. It was really good. Come on Belinda, let's go!"

Belinda didn't budge. "I want to know what's going on with you two."

Joshua stood and pulled Madison close to him. "Mother, meet my future bride." Joshua then looked at Madison nestled against him. "Will you marry me, Madison?"

Madison smiled up at him. "I will."

"So Mother, Dad when Madison and I decide on a date, we'll be married. Is there anything else you'd like to know?"

Belinda glared at them. This couldn't be happening. She looked at the Lindens who had foolish grins on their faces. Had everyone gone mad? Madison was too young for her son. She'd call him later and get to the bottom of this. Could Madison be pregnant?

Dan pulled Belinda up and practically dragged her to the front door. What was wrong with Belinda? She had some explaining to do!

CHAPTER TEN

The Lindens and Joshua stood on the porch until the Cole's truck was out of sight.

Joshua turned to Madison. "I'm sorry I sprung my proposal on you like that." He then spoke to the Linden's, "May I marry your daughter?"

Edward shook Joshua's hand and pulled him in for a hug. "I would be honored to call you son. You're a fine man, Joshua."

It was Joan's turn and she hugged him too. Tears glistened in her eyes as she also hugged her daughter. Madison's prediction was right on and Joan wondered about her insight.

Edward and Joan went inside, leaving Joshua and Madison to themselves. Joshua sat down on the porch swing, and Madison snuggled up next to him.

"Joshua, all my dreams are coming true. Remember when I first met you?"

"Yes, I remember. You were one angry young lady. But I liked your spunk!"

Madison laughed. "I was upset. I didn't want a pony; I wanted a horse. I was so scared when you came along and pushed me into Brandy's stall. A pony looked pretty good about then."

"I was kind of pushy, wasn't I? Guess I thought if you faced your fear, it would help you."

"It did help, Joshua. I needed to walk through this fear, so to speak. Riding has really helped me gain the confidence I lost through the accident." Madison paused. "Joshua, I love you."

Joshua placed his lips gently on hers and sealed his love with a kiss.

CHAPTER ELEVEN

After Dan and Belinda arrived back at their place, Dan demanded sharply, "Okay, Belinda, out with it. What's wrong with you?"

"I don't want to talk about it."

"Well, I want some answers. I've just about had it with your behavior. That stunt you pulled over at the Lindens was embarrassing!"

"Joshua had no right proposing to that girl. He won't talk to me, Dan," pouted Belinda.

"Your apron strings are strangling him, Belinda. You've got to let him go before you lose him completely. I think you better get on your knees and straighten this out before you drive us all out of your life. You think about it, Belinda. I'm going for a ride. Be back later!"

WHEN TWO WORLDS COLLIDE

Belinda felt strange. It was usually her going out the door, but this time Dan beat her to it. She knew pushing Joshua wasn't working. She only wanted the best for her son, why couldn't he see that? They had always been buds, but now she didn't even know who he was. Pastor Blair had better have an explanation for why all the people were leaving the church too. Thinking that talking to him right now might help, Belinda grabbed her Bible and left.

Dan returned from his ride and felt better giving Belinda and the situation to the Lord. Looking through the house and not finding Belinda, Dan hoped she had taken his advice and went to do some soul-searching. He was in his study when a vehicle drove in. Looking out the window and not recognizing the truck, Dan went to the front door. He opened the door before Russ Jacobs had a chance to knock.

"Hey, Russ! Come in. What brings you here?"

"I've got some bad news, Dan."

Dan let Russ in and stood in the entrance way. "What is it?"

"It's Belinda. I think she's lost her mind. I got a call from Ken Blair and it seems Belinda threw a fit at his place. Ken didn't

CHAPTER ELEVEN

want to upset you so he called me. We took her to the hospital, Dan. They've sedated her and for now they've placed her on the psyche ward. I'll take you there if you like."

"Just let me grab my jacket."

Dan was quiet as Russ drove. Oh God, moaned Dan to himself, what's happening to Belinda? She's been acting strangely, and now this. What's wrong?

After seeing Belinda, a nurse took Dan to the doctor's office where he sat down wearily. He was going to ask why Belinda was restrained, but thought he would save his questions for now. She wouldn't hurt anyone, would she? Just then the doctor came in.

"Mr. Cole, I'm Dr. Sherman," he said introducing himself and extending his hand to Dan. "Please, don't get up."

The doctor sat in his chair and looked at Dan. "We're not sure at this point what the diagnosis is for your wife, but we would like to do some tests. Has she been having any headaches?"

Dan thought for a moment. "Occasionally, but what does this have to do with her behavior tonight?"

"That's what I'd like to find out. If you could sign these papers, we'll start them tomorrow morning."

"What kind of tests are you talking about, Doctor?"

"We'll do an MRI. I want to see if there are any blockages." The doctor paused before continuing, "It could also be menopausal, but we'll just have to wait and see."

"All right, Dr. Sherman. I'll sign the papers."

"Mr. Cole, I was just wondering, has Belinda ever had a blow to the head?"

"Yes. It was nineteen years ago, but she was miraculously healed."

"Oh I see. Well that could explain her headaches and her behavior."

"It doesn't explain anything, Dr. Sherman. She was healed," said Dan, annoyed. Wasn't he listening?

"Even after we do the tests, she may be detained further if Ken Blair presses charges," the doctor added sympathetically.

"Charges, what are you talking about? Is Ken Blair in here too?"

"Yes, he's in emergency. They should have him stitched up by now." Doctor Sherman handed Dan some sheets of

CHAPTER ELEVEN

paper and Dan scribbled his name on the bottom of each sheet. "I'll call you after the tests."

"Thanks. Is emergency on the first floor?" asked Dan, his heart now racing once again.

"Yes. I'll take you there if you like."

Dan followed the doctor down the hallway to the elevator. Oh God, breathed Dan, let Pastor Blair be all right.

Dr. Sherman pulled back a curtain and Ken was sitting on the side of the bed.

"Dan, you're here," said Ken, buttoning his shirt. "We need to talk."

"What happened?"

Ken ignored Dan's question. "Do you have your truck here?"

"No, Russ is waiting for me."

"Good, let's get him and go to the church. We've got our work cut out for us."

Dan wanted answers, but Ken seemed to be in his own world. A pain started piercing Dan's chest. What was going on?

After locating Russ, they went to his truck. Once inside, Ken began sharing what had taken place. "Belinda came over to my place and she was very upset. She went on and on about Joshua and Madison. I told her she needed to let go and allow the Lord to handle things. I tried to counsel her and that's when she grabbed a knife from the kitchen and came at me. What was so weird though, is when I looked in her eyes; it wasn't Belinda staring back at me. When she lunged at me, the knife cut my upper arm near my shoulder. I think she was aiming for my heart!"

"Pastor Ken, I'm so sorry. Belinda's been acting strangely for about six months, ever since she found out Joshua is not her son by birth."

"Bingo! You've just hit the problem on the head, Dan. I think that may have been the entry point. Now, we have to get Belinda set free from demonic activity."

"What are you talking about, Pastor Ken?" asked Dan. "Do you think Belinda is possessed?"

"You bet I do! While I was being stitched up, I definitely heard the Lord speaking to me. He even gave me the name of a man He is going to work through to deliver Belinda. His name is Hank Hurley. Ever heard of him?"

"No," said Dan and Russ in unison.

"Well, I'm sure the Lord will give us further direction. Let's do some praying tonight. We're not fighting flesh and blood

CHAPTER ELEVEN

here, but principalities and powers. I'm going to call some people to get praying. This is war!"

Ken was sure fired up thought Dan. He acted like a different man. Then the thoughts of Belinda filled his mind. Oh Belinda, why didn't I see this coming? Dan tried to settle down, but so many questions and scenarios filled his mind.

"Pastor Ken, are you going to press charges?" Dan asked, hesitantly.

"Of course not. Aren't you listening to me? It wasn't Belinda who tried to kill me, it was satan! Don't worry Dan, we'll get Belinda back."

"How do you know all about this demon stuff, Ken?" asked Russ, pulling up to the church. "I've never heard you preach about it."

Ken thought for a moment before he answered. "It's like I've known about it, but never encountered anyone possessed. We all have God's power available to us; we just have to use it. I've decided to take back my authority and calling. I've been pushed around long enough. What I saw in Belinda made me so angry, a righteous anger I guess. We have the authority from Jesus to command these evil beings to get out of our lives. To get us started in this area, the Lord is sending us Hank Hurley to give us some training. So, tonight let's listen to the Lord and do what He says. I think for now He wants us to fast and pray for Belinda. Dan, please call Joshua, he needs to be here."

Dan nodded. What would Joshua think of this? Would he even want to be part of it, after what his mother put him through? He guessed he would know soon enough, as he watched Joshua pull into the church parking lot.

Ken Blair smiled. God had gone ahead and called Joshua too. "Thank you Lord!"

"What's going on?" asked Joshua, as he stood with his dad, Ken, and Russ on the landing of the church steps. "The Lord spoke to me and told me to come here right away."

"Let's go inside," said Ken, "I'll fill you in."

After hearing about the episode, Joshua bowed his head. *"Lord, we need Your help. Thank you for sending Hank Hurley who will teach us about deliverance. We need You to show us how to walk in the Spirit so that nothing we do is of ourselves. Please forgive me for the attitudes I have toward Mom. I repent of my behavior. Thank you for Your forgiveness."*

CHAPTER ELEVEN

"I had quite an experience while staying at your cabin, Dan. A man came by to see me, and now I know it was the Lord. Hey, that's holy ground up there! He spoke some powerful words to me that I see coming to pass right before my eyes," said Ken excitedly. "There is a spiritual world and a physical world. These two worlds are contrary to one another. The physical doesn't fit into the spiritual, but the spiritual realm can fit into the physical realm. We need our minds renewed to know we are spiritual beings; we have a soul and we live in a physical body. Now evil beings have taken up residency in Belinda, but they can't stay. Belinda is a blood-bought child of God. She will be set free. We can count on it! After her deliverance though, she will still have to have the behavioral patterns broken. It will be her decision of course, but we will be here to support and pray for her." Ken beamed with excitement.

Joshua nodded in agreement. "That's exactly right, Pastor Ken. The Lord also showed me with all the miracles taking place in this valley, there will be demonic activity trying to gain ground. But we will not be sidetracked. We know his tactics; we must fight him spirit to spirit."

WHEN TWO WORLDS COLLIDE

Russ and Dan looked at each other.

"I have some spiritual fences to mend then," confessed Russ. "I haven't been reading the Bible or taking my family to church. I don't know where my passion for Jesus went, so I need you fellas to pray for me."

"Forgive me too, Russ, for not being the pastor you needed," added Ken. "I took a permanent vacation when Alice died. I became so self-centered, all I thought about was my grief. I was so glad when the Lord sent Joshua here. He has a special calling on his life."

Dan, Ken, and Joshua stood around Russ and prayed. Each one called out to God for Russ to return to the fold where he would be fed and grow up in Christ. They prayed for him to return to his first love, Christ Jesus. Russ lifted up his arms in surrender and a new light shone through his eyes.

"Thank you, Lord, for Your love! Thank you for not leaving me and bringing me back to You," cried Russ, as tears streamed from his uplifted face.

The group of men let the Lord further minister to each of them. They knew that waiting on the Lord would renew their strength and they would need His strength in the days to

CHAPTER ELEVEN

come. They stayed in agreement until the sun began peeking over the horizon.

Dan broke the silence with, "I'll set up a schedule for my men, and then I'll go over to the hospital to see if I can bring Belinda home."

Russ shocked when he realized what time it was said, "I better get home, Lindsey will wonder what has happened to me."

"She knows, Russ," said Joshua. "I called her earlier and told her what was happening."

"Thanks Joshua. I have a few fences to mend with her too. I'll see you all later."

"So, I can count on you all coming back as soon as Hank Hurley shows up?" asked Ken.

The men nodded in agreement.

Joshua and Dan left the church together. "Mom's going to be all right, Dad," said Joshua, putting his hand on his dad's shoulder.

"I know Josh, but how can these things happen?"

"We live in a pretty messed-up world. It's so important to stay close to the Lord and follow Him closely. I have to run and talk to Madison. I'll also need to do my chores. See you later."

WHEN TWO WORLDS COLLIDE

Dan nodded and watched his son leave. *"Thank you Father, for Your faithfulness!"*

CHAPTER TWELVE

"I was so scared waking up in the hospital, Dan. Why am I here?"

"You don't remember what happened, Belinda?" ask Dan, concerned.

"Do you know, Dan? The only thing I remember is going to Ken's place," sighed Belinda. "Are you here to take me home?"

"We have to see the doctor first and then sign some release papers."

Dan thought Belinda looked quite normal, so may be this deliverance didn't have to take place after all.

A nurse came in just as Dan was about to tell Belinda why she was in the hospital. "The doctor has been called on another emergency. You can sign your wife out, Mr. Cole, but he would like you to bring her in next week."

WHEN TWO WORLDS COLLIDE

Dan looked over the papers and signed them. "I'll call and set up an appointment next week."

The nurse nodded and left the room.

Walking to their vehicle, Belinda looked up at Dan somewhat perplexed. "Dan, I'm fine. Why would I have to come back next week?"

"I don't know, but we'll do what the doctor orders, okay Belinda?"

Belinda seemed lost in her own thoughts on the drive home, which suited Dan just fine. He didn't want to talk right now. This whole thing left him shaking inside.

"I'm going to lie down," announced Belinda when they got home.

"Okay, Belinda, see you when you wake up."

Dan went to his study and rang Pastor Blair's number.

"Hello. Dan, good it's you. You're not going to believe this, but guess who's sitting in my office?"

"Who?"

"Hank Hurley! God sent him here just like He said He would. Could you come over? Hank would like to talk to you."

"I signed Belinda out of the hospital and she's taking a nap right now. Pastor Blair,

CHAPTER TWELVE

Belinda seems quite normal, may be she doesn't need a deliverance."

"Why don't we let Hank be the judge of that, Dan? Belinda looked normal the night she came to see me too."

Dan sighed. "Ask Hank if I can leave her alone."

Dan heard Ken talking and then he came back to the phone. "Yes, she'll be fine. Hank says it's good she's resting."

"I'll be there in a few minutes, Ken."

Dan hung up the phone and then went to their bedroom. Belinda was sound asleep. He tiptoed over to her and kissed her gently on the cheek.

Joshua shifted in his chair as he sat in the administration office of the high school where Madison attended. He stood up when Madison entered the office.

"Joshua, what's wrong?" asked Madison, shocked to see him standing there.

"It's my mom. Let's go somewhere so I can explain."

The secretary looked up from her papers. "Madison, we will need a note

WHEN TWO WORLDS COLLIDE

from your mom, but Pastor Cole has permission to take you out of classes today."

"Okay, thanks."

Joshua took Madison's hand and left the office. "I talked to your principal and the whole school is buzzing about your miracle."

"I know Joshua. I seem to be the main attraction today. Anyway, let's go. I'm curious about your mom."

Joshua pulled up to their church. "This seems a good place to talk. Actually, I'm bringing you here because the Lord spoke to me. He wants you here when Mr. Hurley ministers to my mom."

"So what's wrong with your mom, other than she hates me?"

"She doesn't hate you, satan hates you. It seems Mom needs deliverance. God is sending a man here to minister to her and for some reason, you are to be here as well."

"This is scaring me, Joshua. What do I know about deliverance? I've just come back to the Lord, how can He use me?"

"I was thinking the same thing too Maddie, but the Lord knows what He is doing. Have you been baptized in the Holy Spirit?"

"Yes, when I first asked Jesus into my heart. I had a wonderful experience with Him. He gave me a song to sing in a language I didn't

CHAPTER TWELVE

understand, but then English words came later."

"Madison, you had a beautiful song the Sunday we were at the Applegate Nursing Home."

"Yes. Even though I hadn't rededicated my heart to Him, He spoke and told me to open my mouth and He would fill it. I just obeyed."

"Did you know you could sing like that?"

"No, I didn't Joshua."

A tapping on the window caused Joshua and Madison to stop talking. A man with shoulder-length hair and a full beard looked in at them. Joshua pushed a button and the window opened. "Can I help you?"

"I believe you can, young man. Could you and your lady friend please come into the church?"

The man backed away from the truck to let Joshua and Madison out. Joshua took Madison's hand, and with the man following, they went into the church.

Pastor Ken was in the sanctuary when the three made their entrance. "Good, you're here Joshua. Hello Madison, nice to see you too. Wait a minute, there's something different about you!" exclaimed

WHEN TWO WORLDS COLLIDE

Pastor Ken, puzzled. He looked at her for a few more moments and then began to shout, "You're walking, praise God! You're walking!" He gave Madison a huge hug as tears streamed down his face. "God is truly directing our steps. Joshua, Madison, this is Hank Hurley."

Madison and Joshua shook his hand and then sat down.

"Madison," said Mr. Hurley, "Father God has a special job for you to do while I'm ministering to Mrs. Cole. He wants you to sing. You don't have to worry about what you'll be singing; He'll give you songs of deliverance. The scripture says, *You are my hiding place; You shall preserve me from trouble; You shall surround me with songs of deliverance.*[5]"

"You knew I could sing, Mr. Hurley?"

"Yes, and please call me Hank. We're all God's children and He knows us by name."

"How did you know I could sing?"

"God gives me knowledge about people. He has a purpose and a plan for each one of us. Joshua for instance is anointed by God to preach the gospel and see the captives set free. The Holy Spirit is training him for this calling."

Hank looked over at Joshua. Joshua felt

[5] Psalm 32:7

CHAPTER TWELVE

uncomfortable, Hank's eyes seeming to look right into his soul. "There's some dark times coming, Joshua. You must stay close to Father God."

He glanced back to Madison. "Father is pleased to have you back home."

"I'm thankful to be back."

"I'm also hearing that . . ." Hank paused and listened to a voice no one else could hear. He nodded his head and kept silent.

"Yes?" inquired Madison. "What did the Lord tell you?"

"I'm sorry, I'm not at liberty to speak it right now. Now, Ken, is Dan still coming?"

Just then the door opened and Dan walked in. "Sorry I'm late. Some of the cows broke through a fence and we had to fix it. When I left the house, Belinda was still sleeping."

Hank stood and offered his hand to Dan, "I'm Hank Hurley."

Dan took his hand and smiled. "Nice to meet you." So this is Hank, thought Dan to himself. There was nothing special about the man's appearance except for his eyes. It wasn't so much the color, but the intensity and yet gentleness he saw there.

"Let's begin, shall we?" said Hank, taking a seat beside Joshua.

"Should I go and get Belinda?" asked Dan, somewhat confused.

"No, she's safe with Father and being prepared by Him. We must get our hearts in agreement and co-operate with Him. Madison, when the Holy Spirit gives you a song, sing it forth."

Madison nodded, excitement welling within.

"Father," prayed Hank, *"You know the condition of each heart in this room. We ask for Your divine intervention, for we know we can do nothing without You. We invite You Holy Spirit to search us and reveal the hidden things of our hearts. We give You permission to remove those things hindering our walk with You. We will not hide from You as Adam did in the garden. Your sacrificed Son gives us access into Your presence; and we come boldly before You, Father."*

Dan began to groan. The pressure in his chest seemed unbearable. He slid to his knees and then prostrated himself, hoping to relieve the pressure. In his agony he cried out, "Oh God, forgive me! Forgive me for letting Belinda take headship of our home. I'm a coward, forgive me!"

The thought that 'real men don't cry' flashed through his mind, but he didn't care. The fact was, he was sobbing like a

CHAPTER TWELVE

baby, but the pain was easing in his chest. After the tears stopped, wave upon wave of peace covered him. He slowly moved himself to a kneeling position and raised his arms in praise.

The angelic voice began softly at first, and then rising in volume till the whole building resonated with heavenly notes. The singing carried Dan into the arms of God. He heard the Lord speaking to him through the song, ***"I will never leave you. You can trust Me, My son. I will love you forever. Rest, yes rest in Me."***

The next person to have his face planted on the floor was Joshua. He heard his voice pleading for forgiveness. *"I've been angry with Mom please forgive me! Oh God, being in charge of this congregation has filled me with pride; forgive me! Your Word hasn't been first place; I will eat Your Word before eating anything else. Oh God, I need You! I want You!"*

Ken Blair lay in a crumpled heap on the floor. *"Oh God, have mercy on me, have mercy! I've gone my own way and not listened to Your voice. I've been so rebellious. I've been religious. I've been against You, Holy Spirit. Please forgive me. Please set me free to worship. I need Your power and Your strength. Please fill me with Yourself!"*

WHEN TWO WORLDS COLLIDE

The hours flew past as each soul petitioned the throne room. The sun had long since gone down and the church was dark. Hank found the lights and turned them on.

"Now Dan, you can bring Belinda here," said Hank.

Dan stood, but felt shaky on his feet. "This wasn't about Belinda, was it Hank? It was about our deliverance."

"Dan, we all need to walk humbly before the Lord. He doesn't want us to run off ahead of Him; He wants us to take one step at a time. We need to walk in holiness before Him, asking Him about every detail of our lives. We were bought with a price; we do not belong to ourselves. We belong to Him. The world wants us to think like them, but we have been born-again. We are not of this world even though we live here. Our minds must be renewed with the Word of God because the Word is living. The Word knows we need help. The Word is for our spirit, soul and body. We make things complicated, the world makes things complicated, but God simply wants us to understand that He will look after us. *He says when our ways please Him, He will even make our enemies to be at peace with us.*[6]"

Hank looked at everyone. "You will be trained in righteousness. You've had a

[6] Proverbs 16:7

CHAPTER TWELVE

taste of God, so hunger and thirst for Him daily. Many things will try and distract you, so you must press on."

Hank turned back to Dan. "Go get Belinda. We will stay in an attitude of prayer and praise."

"Why do we get so side-tracked, Hank?" asked Ken.

"Sometimes it's fear of man. You, for instance, are a people pleaser and God will change that in you. You should take your instructions from God and let the Lord deal with the people."

"You're right. I just don't like to rock the boat. I've tried to be a good pastor."

"That won't cut it, Ken. You won't be rocking the boat because you won't be in the boat. The Lord wants you to walk with Him. Some things He will be instructing you to say will be hard, but victory and freedom are just around the corner for many in this congregation. I would seriously think about a building program; you're going to need a bigger building for the people the Lord will send you."

Hank turned to Joshua. "You're called of God. Pride will rear its ugly head, so you must be constantly on guard. Mighty signs and wonders will follow you, Joshua. Even though you'll be in some dark places, God will be with you."

Hank then went over and took Madison by the hand. "I can now speak what I couldn't say earlier. You're life here on earth will be short. God has given you a specific job to do, then He will be calling you home."

Startled Madison looked at Joshua, tears starting to collect in her eyes. Joshua put his arm around her. "Hank, you're scaring her."

"It's not a scary thing to go home to heaven, Joshua," explained Hank. "We are strangers here; our destination is heaven."

"But Madison just turned eighteen. She can't be going home yet, can she?"

"Time is in God's hands, so I don't question Him."

Joshua led Madison to the back of the church and sat down with her.

"I think we should get married on Sunday with our church family in attendance," said Joshua, concerned with what Hank had said.

"I have a peace, Joshua. If God wants us to marry, then we'll be married. I've always wanted to be your wife," said Madison, looking up at Joshua shyly.

CHAPTER TWELVE

Joshua took Madison's trembling hand. "Will you marry me on Sunday, Madison?"

Madison let tears fall from her eyes unhindered. "Yes, Joshua Cole, I will."

Joshua pulled Madison toward him and hugged her.

"I just thought of something Joshua. I don't have a wedding dress," said Madison. She thought for a moment and then added, "I could wear my new prom dress, I guess."

"You could wear jeans, for all I care!"

"Oh Joshua, I wouldn't wear jeans. I wonder, though, what Mom and Dad will say to all of this."

"We'll explain everything to them later, Madison, and don't worry."

"This is the strangest thing, Joshua, I'm not worried. This feels so right!"

CHAPTER THIRTEEN

Dan found Belinda arousing from her sleep. It had to have been the Lord keeping her asleep, for he had been away for six hours.

"Dan," said Belinda groggily, "how long have I been sleeping?"

"For awhile Belinda, but now we have to see someone."

"I don't want to see anyone. I'll make you a nice dinner and we'll start a fire. Just the two of us."

Not wanting to rile her, Dan replied, "That'll be nice Belinda, but Pastor Blair needs us at the church."

"He wants to see me?" asked Belinda, looking bewildered.

"Just for a little while. I told him we would be right over."

Belinda hesitated. "Well, okay, if it's just

for a little while. I thought he was angry with me."

"Why would you say that?"

"I don't know, just a feeling I get."

Was Belinda remembering what had happened? Dan decided not to pursue any line of questioning with her. Soon everything would be in the light. Dan escorted Belinda to their truck, inwardly thanking the Lord for all that was going to take place.

Once at the church, Belinda cringed. "What are all these vehicles doing here? I thought you said only Pastor Blair wanted to see us."

"It's all right Belinda, let's just go in."

"No, Dan Cole, I will not leave this truck. You tell Pastor Blair to come out here!"

"Come on Belinda, don't be childish, Pastor Blair is waiting for us."

"Forget it, Dan, and I'm not being childish. What are you up to, anyway?"

Dan hesitated. May be he should go in and get Hank, but then again he didn't want to leave Belinda alone, not knowing what she would do. He then apologized to the Lord for his next statement, "I think the worship team is practicing songs for Sunday. We'll be in the pastor's office, so come on, let's not keep the pastor waiting."

CHAPTER THIRTEEN

Belinda reluctantly opened her door. Something inside her was screaming no! Don't go into the church! Dan came around to help her out. She leaned up against him and could barely take a step. What was going on? Dan put his arm around her and then thought he should may be carry her, when she suddenly stepped back.

A deep guttural voice spoke from Belinda, "I will not leave! I've been invited and I will not leave."

Hank seemed to appear out of nowhere and stood in front of Belinda. "Yes, you will leave. You have no place in this child of God." Hank's voice was even-toned, yet carried much authority.

Belinda slumped against Dan and he quickly supported her by lifting her into his arms. Hank opened the church door and Dan followed him in. He carefully laid Belinda down on the floor near the podium and stood back. Belinda began writhing, seemingly being tormented from within.

Hank motioned to Madison to begin singing and everyone else began to pray.

"You vile, corrupt beings, I speak to you in the mighty name of Christ Jesus. Come out of her!"

WHEN TWO WORLDS COLLIDE

    A smell of rotting eggs filled the sanctuary. With one last jerk and a groan, the evil beings left and went back to the dry places where the man of God sent them.

    With a surprised look on her face, Belinda slowly sat up. She then knelt and cried out to God, "Please forgive me! I give you my life and total control. I desire to do those things pleasing to You."

    Madison continued to sing and suddenly an aroma of roses filled the sanctuary. It sounded like many voices lifting praises to the Lord. Encouraged Madison allowed the Holy Spirit to sing through her, hitting notes she knew were humanly impossible.

    Hank knelt beside Belinda. "Your children are with the Lord. He will give you other children, Belinda, spiritual children to disciple and train. He is calling you to be a mother to many."

    "Yes, I know, He showed me my children. They're safe with Him. I'll do whatever He wants me to do."

    Hank helped Belinda to her feet and hugged her. "I know Belinda, you have a desire to follow after Him and He will never let you go."

    Belinda then noticed the other people in the room. She practically ran to Joshua.

CHAPTER THIRTEEN

"Oh, Joshua, please forgive me."

"I forgive you mom, and will you forgive me? I shouldn't have let my anger control me."

"I forgive you, but I was the one with all the anger." Belinda then noticed Madison. She slowly walked over to her. "I'm so sorry for my behavior, Madison. Will you forgive me?"

"Yes, Mrs. Cole, I forgive you."

Joshua came and stood with Madison. "Maddie and I are getting married on Sunday, Mom."

"You're what? Getting married on Sunday?" asked Belinda with disbelief, "you've got to be kidding. There won't be enough time to plan a wedding!"

"We don't need to plan anything, Mrs. Cole. I don't want a big wedding, I only want to spend the rest of my days with Joshua."

"What do you mean, the rest of your days, Madison? You'll have a lifetime together," replied Belinda.

"I don't know how many days I'll have, Mrs. Cole," said Madison, not wanting to upset her with Hank's prediction. "I just want to spend each day with Joshua."

"Do your mom and dad know?" questioned Belinda.

"Not yet, but we'll tell them tonight."

"I guess I don't want you two rushing into this relationship without knowing one another," added Belinda.

"Okay, Mother, let me ask you a question. How long did you know Dad before you married him?"

Belinda glanced over at Dan and smiled. "I see where you're going with this, Joshua. I guess for as long as you've known Madison. But we've had our struggles . . . you know that."

Not letting up, Joshua asked, "And how old were you, when you married, Mom?"

"I was seventeen, Joshua."

Joshua put his arm around Madison. "Look, I'm not trying to compare your situation with mine, Mom, but Madison and I are meant for each other, and we don't want to wait."

Belinda walked over and took Dan's arm. "What do you think, Dan?"

"I think we better order a cake!"

Everyone burst into laughter. Joshua turned to Hank, "Will you stay and come to our marriage?"

"I'll have to check with my boss and get back to you," smiled Hank.

"If you're staying Hank, please come to

CHAPTER THIRTEEN

our house," invited Belinda. "You can have Joshua's room."

"That's very kind of you, Belinda. If I stay, I'll get Ken to bring me over to your place."

Belinda then walked up to Ken.

"Pastor Ken, what happened after I came to see you the other day?" asked Belinda.

"You weren't yourself Belinda. It wasn't you who attacked me, it was the evil beings."

"I attacked you?" asked Belinda, totally shocked.

"Yes, with a knife, Belinda. But don't worry . . . they stitched me up at the hospital, and I'll be fine."

"Stitches, you had stitches? I'm so sorry," said Belinda, tears collecting in her eyes.

Ken came and put his arms around her. "It's all right, Belinda. I'll live. It'll take more than a few stitches to put me down. I'm so thankful for your deliverance and freedom."

Belinda looked up at him. "I'm so thankful too, Pastor Ken."

Presently everyone left and Ken went to his office to retrieve some books. Hank followed him.

"I really thought the deliverance would take longer," mused Ken, as he shuffled through some papers on his desk.

WHEN TWO WORLDS COLLIDE

"The authority we have is because Jesus gave it to us before He left. Do you remember what He said in Mark, *and these signs will follow those who believe: In My name they will cast out demons; they will speak with new tongues.*[7] And also in Mark, near the end of the verse, *for with authority He commands even the unclean spirits, and they obey Him.*[8] These evil spirits do not obey man. They obey God. These spirits know we have been given authority, we just have to believe."

"Why do you think it takes some people longer to see the evil spirits leave then?"

"I don't care to speculate on this Ken. I just do what I see Jesus doing in His word."

Ken smiled. "You certainly live the Word Hank, you certainly do. Now will you need a ride to the Coles'?"

"I'd like to stay a little longer in the church if you don't mind Ken. I'll lock the doors when I leave, is it all right with you?"

"That'll be fine Hank. I'm so glad God sent you to us. We have so much to learn. I hope the Lord lets you stay on so you can teach us a thing or two."

"As you study, Ken, I believe God will use you to teach these people. You already have the gift of teaching, and the

[7] Mark 16:17
[8] Mark 1:27

CHAPTER THIRTEEN

Holy Spirit, who teaches you all things, will help you."

Ken reached for Hank's outstretched hand. Ken didn't want to let go of this man of God.

CHAPTER FOURTEEN

"Your folks actually took the news of our up coming marriage quite well, don't you think, Madison?"

Madison looked up at Joshua and began thanking the Lord for all of her dreams coming true. She would be going to high school next week as Mrs. Madison Cole. What would her classmates think? They were now on their way to pick out rings. Excitement bubbled up and Madison thought she could scream with the intensity of it.

"I think they were a little startled," replied Madison, "but they've always wanted my happiness. I think they trust you, Joshua, to make me happy."

"I'll do my best Maddie, but you and I know it's only the Lord who can bring us true happiness."

WHEN TWO WORLDS COLLIDE

"Can you believe I will be Madison Kathleen Cole tomorrow, Joshua?"

Joshua held on to the wheel with one hand and put his arm around Madison, squeezing her closer to him. He looked at Madison for only a moment, then the sound of screeching brakes and crushing metal was all he heard. Blackness filled his world and then all was quiet.

Dan picked up the ringing phone and Edward's panicked voice filled him with dread. "There's been a terrible accident! It's Joshua and Madison! They've been taken to the General hospital. We'll meet you there." Then there was an abrupt click.

"Oh God, no! Belinda, hurry, we have to go to the hospital. Josh and Madison have been in an accident!" Dan tried to be still, but waves of fear engulfed him.

The Coles rushed into the emergency where they met up with the Lindens. They were both sobbing and holding each other. "Our baby, she's gone, she's gone!"

Dan and Belinda trembled with fear. They surrounded the Lindens and cried with

CHAPTER FOURTEEN

them. Finally Dan had the courage to ask, "What about Joshua?"

Edward gripped Dan's arm and tried to reply, "They're still working on him."

Just then a doctor came into the room. "Who are the parents of the young man?"

"We are," replied Dan and Belinda together.

"His head injuries are severe and he's in a coma. We have him on life-support. Now we wait. You can see him now. Come this way."

The Lindens went sat down while the Coles followed the doctor out of the room. The doctor then turned and spoke softly to them. "Your son was wearing a seat belt which probably saved his life. The young girl wasn't and was projected from the vehicle, killing her instantly." The doctor left them staring at their son, tubes and wires protruding from his still form. Joshua had a few cuts and bruises on his face, but other than that he looked intact. Belinda took his hand and began to cry. *"Father,"* she pleaded, *"You know the outcome of all things. We give you Joshua and trust You to look after him. Please give him back to us."*

Dan continued to stare at Joshua and then knew he had a phone call to make. "I'll be right back, Belinda, there's someone I need to call."

WHEN TWO WORLDS COLLIDE

Belinda nodded. Yes, Peter and Stacey, Dan's brother and sister-in-law, will want to come and Pastor Ken will need to be notified, thought Belinda when Dan left. She pulled up a chair closer to the bed to continue her vigil.

After all the connections were made, Dan had his party on the line. "Doug Shriver? This is Dan Cole from Montana."

"Hello Dan, how can I help you?"

Dan paused trying to slow down his racing heart. "There's been a terrible accident. Your son, Joshua, and his fiancée were in a serious car crash. She was killed and Joshua is in a coma. I thought you and Cynthia would want to know."

"I'm so sorry to hear this. Can we come?"

"I thought you might like to. We're at the General hospital in Billings."

"Thanks for calling, Dan. We'll get a flight out as soon as possible and meet you there."

"Okay great. My wife, Belinda, and I will be here as we want to stay close to Joshua."

Dan hung up the phone and breathed a prayer. *"I hope I did the right thing."*

CHAPTER FOURTEEN

Joshua found himself lying in a meadow on the greenest grass he had ever seen. There was a face peering down at him so he sat up to see Madison pulling on his hand. "Come on Joshua, this place is heavenly! There's so much to see!"

Joshua felt light permeate his body and he had an incredible sense of joy. Madison looked radiant! Her white dress flowed with each step, and her silky blond hair bounced about her shoulders. He reached out and took some strands in his fingers. Yes, it was as silky as it looked. "Madison, you're so beautiful. I'm so thankful God gave you to me."

Madison laughed. "Joshua, you're my dream come true! We'll be able to spend eternity together. Come on, I want to show you something."

Still holding Joshua's hand, Madison led him through a wooded area to a stream, which seemed to sparkle and dance with movement. They followed it along until the banks grew wider and soon it was a river. On the other side, a tall figure was motioning for them to come. Without hesitation,

WHEN TWO WORLDS COLLIDE

Madison jumped in. She didn't seem to be swimming although the water was covering her. Madison called to Joshua, "Come on, this is glorious! You can even breathe in this water, it's amazing!"

Joshua went to put his foot in when he felt a hand on his shoulder. A voice softly spoke, "Not yet, Joshua."

Joshua turned to the voice and found Hank Hurley standing there. "Why can't I go with Maddie?"

"It's not your time, Joshua. There are still things the Father wants you to do on earth."

Puzzled, Joshua asked, "Is this heaven?"

"Yes, but only a small part of heaven."

Joshua stared after Madison who was already on the other side standing with the tall form. "Joshua," called out Madison, "I'll see you soon!"

Joshua's heart sank. He waved only because she waved and then she was gone. He turned back to Hank, "So if this is heaven, how did you get here?"

"Joshua, you know we are spirit beings. We can come freely here and sometimes the Father even lets us cross the river. This is our place of refreshing. We come here to bask in His Presence to receive anointing

CHAPTER FOURTEEN

for our work on earth. But we must go now, your parents are coming to see you."

Somehow Joshua knew it wasn't Dan and Belinda Hank was talking about. "Are we having an out-of-body experience, Hank?"

Hank laughed. "I guess you could call it that."

Joshua felt tremendous joy and sadness all at the same time. He would miss Madison, but knowing he would one day be with her again eased the ache in his heart.

"If this is real, Hank, where are all the other saints?"

Deep in thought, Hank answered carefully, "There are so many who do not believe this is available for them to walk in now. Remember what Jesus said, ***"Let not your heart be troubled, you believe in God, believe also in Me. In My Father's house are many mansions, if it were not so, I would have told you. I go to prepare a place for you. And if I go to prepare a place for you, I will come again and receive you to Myself that where I am, there you may be also. And where I go you know, and the way you know."***[9] As I meditated on this scripture, He showed me this place where I can come and go. We

[9] John 14:1-4

need to keep seeking Joshua, and we will find. He has promised us!"

"I've never looked at the scriptures this way before, Hank. The way you explain them, they are living! So, what you're saying then, is I can come and see Madison anytime I want?"

"I'm not saying you will always see Madison, Joshua, but you will see God!"

"I'm ready to . . ." started Joshua.

Joshua's mouth was dry and the words he formed in his mind didn't come out of his mouth. He slowly opened his eyes and two strangers stared back at him. Tears welled in their eyes as they stepped back. Joshua blinked again and saw Dan and Belinda.

"Joshua, you're back!" cried Belinda, taking his hand and squeezing it.

His body felt sluggish, but he tried to lift his head. A white coat came into view and a man put a hand on his shoulder. "Easy does it, you've been sleeping for two weeks; don't try to do too much. Glad to see you are awake." The doctor looked with a bright light into Joshua's eyes and

CHAPTER FOURTEEN

then tested other parts of his body. Joshua felt he could get up right away, but allowed the pushing and prodding. "We'll do some further tests tomorrow, but for now get some rest."

Joshua smiled. Wasn't two weeks enough rest? He felt one hundred per cent. Joshua scanned the room and noticed Dan and Belinda, but didn't recognize the other two people.

Dan came over with the strangers. "Josh, this is Doug and Cynthia Shriver."

Joshua smiled. They looked like nice people, though he had imagined them to be older.

"It's nice to meet you, Joshua," said Cynthia, reaching over and taking Joshua's hand. "I'm sorry we had to meet you like this, but we're glad your dad called us."

Dan moved back over to Belinda and let the couple meet their son.

Joshua wanted to speak, but his tongue seemed to be glued to the roof of his mouth. He smiled hoping they knew he was glad to meet them too. Suddenly his thoughts went to Madison and his heart began to ache. He missed her so much. He needed to find out how the accident happened.

WHEN TWO WORLDS COLLIDE

"You don't need to talk, Joshua, we're just happy you're still here so we can get to know you," said Doug reaching for Joshua's other hand.

Belinda watched the interaction and her heart burned. At first when Dan had told her whom he called, she was upset. But as she thought about it, it was the right decision to make. If she had been in their position, she would have wanted to know, too. The Shrivers were a wonderful couple and she just knew they would be friends. Knowing they didn't want to break up their family, gave Belinda a peace in her heart. As soon as Joshua was up to it, she sensed he would go to Canada and spend time with them. She then lifted her concerns to her Heavenly Father and thanked Him for what He was going to do.

CHAPTER FIFTEEN

After going through all the tests the doctor had prescribed, Joshua sat on the edge of his bed waiting to be released from the hospital. He hoped the Shrivers wouldn't be picking him up, as he wanted to be with his own family right now. Joshua stared out of the window and thought about the Lindens. What must they be going through, when his own heart ached with the loss of Madison? He had heard they came to see him when he was still in a coma, but not since he awoke. Were they wishing it was he who had died and not their only child? Joshua was eager to share with them how he was with Madison and how happy she actually was. A knock on his door brought him back from his thoughts. Joshua stood up slowly, "Come in."

Joan and Edward Linden stepped through the door and Joshua walked over and embraced them.

WHEN TWO WORLDS COLLIDE

Edward spoke first. "I hope you don't mind if we came to pick you up Joshua; we'd like to take you to where we buried Madison."

Tears collected in Joshua's eyes and he didn't try to rub them away. "I'd like that," he said softly.

Joshua stood with the Lindens at Madison's grave. He soon slumped to his knees as grief overcame him. He missed her terribly, but he knew she was so happy where she was that he felt cheated he couldn't be with her. After some time, Joshua slowly got up and leaned against Edward. "She would have been a beautiful bride," whispered Joshua. "I need to tell you what happened when I was in the coma. I was with Madison."

"Really, Joshua," Edward and Joan said in unison, astonished at his statement.

"You saw our Madison?" questioned Joan. "How, where?"

They found a bench near Madison's grave and the Lindens listened in awe to Joshua's story.

"I didn't know where I was. I was lying on the most beautiful grass I had ever seen. Madison was looking down at me. She told me to follow her. She was so beautiful." Joshua paused as the memory

CHAPTER FIFTEEN

of his experience began to overwhelm him. "Her dress flowed with each step and her hair shone like gold. She took me to a stream that grew wider as we walked along its bank until it became a river. The whole time she laughed and giggled like a little girl. Suddenly she jumped into the river and called for me to join her. The water was over her head and she said she could breathe in it. It was fascinating. I was just about to take the plunge when a person stopped me. He said it wasn't my time. When I looked for Madison again she was already on the other side standing with a man who I believe was Jesus. When I was in that place . . . nothing here on earth can be compared to it. Joan, Edward, there is a place called heaven! It is real!"

Joan took a deep breath and her tears rolled down her cheeks unhindered. "The Lord gave me a dream too, Joshua. He showed me Maddie and she was wearing the dress you talked about. She was radiant. I know I'll see her someday, too."

Joshua shook his head. "No, Joan, you don't understand, this wasn't a dream, and I was really there. I didn't say anything before, but the man who stopped me from going to join Madison was Hank Hurley. He was the one involved with Mom's deliverance."

WHEN TWO WORLDS COLLIDE

"How can this be, Joshua?" asked Edward.

"I don't know. I found it hard to believe when I was right there. I'll be looking up instances in the scriptures where people have been translated and I'll let you know."

Joan and Edward put their arms around Joshua. "We'd consider it an honor if you stayed part of our family, Joshua."

Joshua could only nod as their love seeped into his grieving heart. After some time, Joshua asked his dreaded question. "Could you please tell me how the accident happened?"

"Well," began Edward, "a trucker who had been on a long haul fell asleep at the wheel. He walked away from the accident without a scratch. He's been charged with driving with undo care and attention . . . involuntary manslaughter, they called it. But with all that goes on in our justice system these days, I'm sure he'll walk away from this too," said Edward bitterly. "One thing we can't understand though Joshua, is why wasn't Madison wearing her seat belt?"

Joshua cringed. "It was my fault. I asked her to come closer to me and by the time I thought about the lap seat belt it was too late. I'm so sorry."

CHAPTER FIFTEEN

"We needed to know, Joshua. It would have may be helped if she was wearing a seat belt, but with the impact you sustained, we're not sure. I guess it was her time, Joshua, because you took the same impact, and here you are." Edward paused before continuing. "We better get you home. I took Blaze back to your place and I've been looking after your other stock for you. And Josh, I have an extra vehicle you can use until you get another one."

"Thanks Edward, I'd appreciate that. Could you take me to my parents place? I don't want to be alone right now." Joshua looked at them both. "Please forgive me for not looking after your daughter like I said I would."

"We forgive you, Joshua," answered Joan. "It will take time, though, for our hearts to stop aching."

Joshua nodded. "I know Joan, I know."

"I hope it was all right for the Lindens to pick you up, Joshua; they were quite insistent," said Belinda, adding another plate to the table. "We thought you'd be longer, so we weren't expecting you for dinner."

"I knew I would have to face them sooner or later."

"Did it go badly?"

"No, but I'm alive and their only daughter is dead. I wish I could be with Madison."

Belinda stopped what she was doing and looked at her son. "I'm glad you're here, Joshua. You have a special anointing on your life and God needs you here."

"You haven't been talking to Hank, have you?"

"No, why do you ask?"

"He said about the same thing you're saying, Mom." Changing the subject, Joshua added, "I loved Maddie and I felt the Lord saying I could marry her."

Belinda came over and put her arms around Joshua. "I know, but accidents happen. It's not your fault and it's not God's fault. Accidents just happen. Josh, I'm really sorry about Madison. When I finally came to my senses, I knew . . . she was the woman for you."

Joshua smiled. "Thanks Mom, even though you thought she was too young for me?"

"She was young, Joshua, but I could see the love you had for each other. I just didn't want you to go through all the trials your dad and I went through getting married so young."

"Well, you won't have to worry about that now. May be I'll become a priest and

CHAPTER FIFTEEN

you won't have to worry about who I marry."

Belinda frowned, not taking what Joshua said with the humor that was intended.

"You'll marry, Joshua. The Lord gave me a vision of your children."

"That's nice Mom. How many children do I have?"

"I can see you're not taking me seriously. I'll keep that to myself until the time is right to share it."

Joshua stepped back from Belinda. "Sorry, Mom, but I don't want to think about another woman. I don't think my heart has room for anyone but Madison." The thought of Madison caused his heart to ache again so he changed the subject. "The Shrivers want me to accompany them on their next mission trip. Did they tell you?"

"Yes, to a mission in Tijuana. Did you think about going?"

"I told them I would let them know. They seem like a nice couple."

"Yes, Joshua, they're very nice people."

"I guess I have two sisters. I'm not sure what to think about that."

"I find it difficult to get used to the idea of your other family too, Joshua. I'm praying the Lord will give you strength to bond with them."

Joshua took a deep breath. "I just want to be friends with them, Mom. I already have my own family."

Belinda stepped into Joshua's outstretched arms. "Thank you, Joshua. I love you so much."

CHAPTER SIXTEEN

"He's a Blazen'" pranced around the corral snorting, his head lifted high. Leaning against the fence, Joshua looked on with amusement. Blaze saw his visitor and came over to investigate. He allowed Joshua to stroke his neck and face. "I'll take you for a ride later, boy. I'd like to see what you can do out on the wide open prairie."

"May be we can go for ride together," said a voice from behind Joshua, startling him.

Joshua turned around. "Hank, what are you doing here?"

"I have some unfinished business to take care of."

"It isn't Mom, is it?"

"No."

"Let's go to the house and I'll fix you some coffee." Joshua thought for a moment and then added, "You do drink coffee don't you?"

"No, but a glass of lemonade would hit the spot."

"Coming right up!"

Joshua and Hank settled in on the front porch. Hank was the first to speak. "Do you know me, Joshua?"

"Yes."

"I mean, we knew each other before I met you at the church."

"I usually remember people, Hank, and I don't ever remember meeting you before," said Joshua, puzzled by this line of questioning.

"You really don't recognize me?"

Joshua looked pensively at Hank and shook his head, "Sorry, can't say as I do."

Hank paused and took a deep breath. "My name is Hank Hurley Pool."

"What? No! I mean, you can't be. Hank is stationed in Hawaii with the Navy. You don't look like him at all."

"I've never wanted to reveal my real identity since I was healed and delivered. But now I sense the Lord wants me to face my parents once again. This is a long story, but I feel I need to talk to you about it. First of all, thank you for being obedient to visit

CHAPTER SIXTEEN

my mom and dad. You were instrumental in opening the door of their hearts to the power of God." Hank shifted in his chair and continued. "As you know Joshua, I was such a rebel. You and I got into some trouble, but when I left here, I took rebellion to the limit. I was involved with drugs, alcohol and sexual affairs. After I joined the Navy, I got involved with this guy and then brought him home to meet Mom and Dad."

Joshua stared blankly at Hank, not knowing what to say.

"It's okay Josh, don't say anything. Like I said before I have to tell you this. Anyway, deep down inside I knew how Mom and Dad would react, but I didn't care. I wanted to hurt them for all their strict attitudes and not loving me the way I needed to be loved. It turned out worse than I expected. Dad went into a rage and physically threw me out of the house. He yelled at me that I wasn't his son and as far as he was concerned I was dead. Mom stood with him and told me to change my last name. She didn't want anyone to know I was a Pool. So I yelled right back and called them every name I could think of. It was an ugly scene. When I arrived back at base this guy and I parted ways. He was suddenly transferred which suited me just fine. I decided then to change my sexual preferences, but all my other behavioral patterns stayed the same. I started getting really sick Joshua, and after going to the doctor on base, he diagnosed me with AIDS. I was very fearful." Hank took another sip from his lemonade and continued, "The Navy discharged me so I traveled to San Francisco, rented an apartment and waited to die. I was flipping through the channels one night and a man in a white suit looked right into the camera at me. He said there was a young man somewhere out there watching who was dying from AIDS. He pointed his finger at the camera and said God was healing him. Joshua, a fire started burning within me. I fell to my knees and began to cry out to a God I didn't know. Suddenly, I knew I was healed. It seemed in a moment I went from darkness to light. I met Jesus Christ face to face and I knew this world was no longer my home. I was born again! I began to devour the words in His book, The Holy Bible. It was more than a book; it was living bread, manna from heaven! The Holy Spirit began teaching and training me. He now sends me all over the world. Before I came to Montana, He told me I needed to be

CHAPTER SIXTEEN

reconciled with my parents. I know He has gone on ahead of me to make all the crooked places straight."

Joshua sat spellbound and could hardly breathe, hearing this powerful testimony. Hank was a different man. It was no wonder he hadn't recognized him. Hank was truly a new creation, filled with the power and anointing of God. "I'd like to come with you when you meet with your mom and dad, Hank. I've witnessed firsthand the transformation of your mom and dad. They're different people too."

Hank smiled. "I was hoping you would come with me. I need a healing with my parents."

Conrad and Ethel Pool were sitting on their veranda when Joshua's truck pulled into the yard.

"Good, Joshua is here," said Conrad, "and he's brought a friend."

Ethel and Conrad stayed seated until their guests came to them. Ethel felt her heart begin to race when she looked at the young man with Joshua. Why did he

WHEN TWO WORLDS COLLIDE

look so familiar? Ethel kept staring, could it be . . .? Ethel glanced over at her husband and he had the same bewildered look. They both stood up and moved towards the young man.

"Hank? Hank, is that you?" cried Ethel.

Hank didn't know what to do. Should he just come out and say yes or wait until his mom spoke again. *Father what . . .?*

The next thing he knew his mom and dad were hugging him until it was hard to breathe.

Conrad spoke first, "You were dead and now you are alive. Welcome home, son!"

Tears ran freely. Even Joshua was caught up in the emotional homecoming.

Once inside the house, Ethel went to check on the dinner she had cooking. Hank and Joshua sat on the couch while Conrad took the armchair across the room from them. Ethel came into the living room and stared at Hank. "What took you so long to come home?" she wondered.

"I've dreaded coming back here after the way I treated you both. Mom, Dad, will you forgive me?"

"Yes," they said in unison.

Ethel came over and took Hank's hand in hers. "And will you forgive us for not giving

CHAPTER SIXTEEN

you the love and attention you needed? We were wrong too, Hank. We were just too bullheaded and ignored all the signs. Our hearts were hard towards the Lord as well. But He did get our attention one day and we've had a homecoming of our own." Ethel smiled at Conrad and joined him by sitting on the arm of his chair. They took each other's hands and beamed. "God is teaching us how to love. But first we had to accept His love for us. It's really hard to give out love if you don't think you're loved."

"Exactly," smiled Hank. "His commandments set us free as we obey Him in all we say and do."

"I'm glad you didn't change your name, Hank," said Ethel with a twinkle in her eye.

"I'll always be a Pool, Mom. I needed something to hold on to in all the mess I found myself in. But that's in the past now, covered by the blood of Christ. I'm so thankful the Lord brought me to this valley, for He has brought me full circle. Would you mind if I stayed with you for a few days? I haven't heard where my next assignment is yet."

"You're welcomed here anytime, son," said Conrad.

Ethel beamed in agreement. She was excited at the prospect of having Hank all to themselves. "We have so much catching up to do." Ethel looked over at Joshua. "Please stay and have dinner with us."

"That would be great. It smells pretty good in here."

"Joshua," began Conrad, "we're so sorry to hear about Madison Linden. How are you holding up?"

Just the sound of her name brought a pang of loneliness into Joshua's heart. "I miss her, but I know she's happy where she is. Her homecoming was an awesome sight!"

"I'm sure it was, Joshua. One day we will see Christ face to face, and what a day that will be!"

Before going into the kitchen for dinner, Conrad turned to his son and put his arms around him. "Welcome home, Hank!"

Tears sprang to Hank's eyes, "It's good to be home, Dad."

CHAPTER SEVENTEEN

Dan dialed his brother's number and his sister-in-law, Stacey, picked up on the other end.

"Hi Dan, it's so nice to hear from you." Just then Emily began to whimper. "Just a minute, while I put Emily down."

Dan waited, listening to the baby, now crying loudly.

"Why does this happen the moment I get on the phone," said Stacey, agitated with the interruption.

Dan smiled. "Brings back memories, Stacey; Joshua used to do that too. I guess it's because they want our total attention at all times. Anyway, Stacey, is Peter there?"

"No, sorry. He's out on a call."

"Could you please tell him to give me a call when he comes in?"

"Is there something I can help you with?"

"No, just wanted to touch base with him is all."

"Okay. We were wondering, how Joshua is doing after his accident?"

"He's home and is doing quite well. It's a miracle he's still with us, as his fiancée died in the accident."

"Yes, we were so sorry to hear it, Dan. How's Belinda doing?"

Something in Stacey's tone of voice bothered him. "Really good, why do you ask?"

"Peter told me what you shared with him about Belinda. She needs deliverance Dan. May be we could come and minister to her."

For some reason Dan felt condemnation coming from Stacey and it troubled him. "She's already been delivered, Stacey. The Lord sent a man to us and through his ministry, she was totally set free."

"Oh really? What's his name?"

"Hank Hurley."

"Oh no! Please tell me you didn't let that man touch Belinda, Dan!"

"What do you mean? Do you know Hank?"

"Not personally, I've just heard some disturbing things about his tactics. I sure wouldn't want him anywhere near me."

CHAPTER SEVENTEEN

Dan took a deep breath. "I don't think you've heard the right things then, Stacey. Hank moves powerfully in the Spirit. I don't think I've met anyone who is closer to the Lord than he is."

"I'll get Peter to call you, Dan," said Stacey abruptly. "Emily is crying again so I need to look after her."

Dan heard a click and he put the phone back into its cradle. Funny, he hadn't heard Emily crying. Dan poured himself a cup of coffee and sat at the kitchen table.

Belinda came into the kitchen and joined him.

"I just called Peter and he wasn't there, so I talked to Stacey for a few minutes. She certainly was agitated."

"So what's new, Dan? I'm sorry to be so critical, but there's something wrong with that lady."

"I think you're right, Belinda. She was quite upset when I told her about Hank."

"Really, does she know him?"

"She said she didn't, she just heard things about him."

"Hmmm. Well, I know God sent him here and personally, I'm glad he came. Those things in me seemed to know Hank quite well."

WHEN TWO WORLDS COLLIDE

Dan looked at Belinda. Yes, she certainly was changing. Some of her behavioral patterns were still evident, but as soon as they came to the surface, Belinda handed them over to the Lord. Through Hank's ministry, he knew a change had happened in him. He continually desired closeness to the Lord and wanted to move in the Spirit like Hank did. Hank shared that each child of God could walk in the Spirit and experience His fullness day to day.

"You look deep in thought, Dan. What were you thinking?"

"How blessed we are with Hank coming here. His ministry was for me too. I long to be close to the Lord, like Hank is."

"I want that too, Dan. Are you still going to invite Stacey and Peter to come?"

"Now more than ever, Belinda. I believe they need to be set free, too."

Belinda knew she had forgiven Stacey, but the test would be to love her through Christ.

A truck pulling a horse trailer, coming into the yard, caused Belinda and Dan to look out the window.

"It's Joshua and Hank. Whose truck is he driving?" wondered Belinda aloud.

As the two men approached the

CHAPTER SEVENTEEN

house, Dan opened the back door for them.

Dan ushered them into the kitchen and Belinda greeted them first. She hugged Joshua, but didn't know about hugging Hank. He put her at ease by hugging her first.

"I thought you would be out on another mission by now Hank," said Dan, finding a chair beside Belinda.

Joshua poured himself a coffee and topped up Dan and Belinda's cups. He then poured Hank a glass of juice.

"I needed to see my parents before I left, Dan."

"You have family in this area, Hank?" asked Belinda, sipping her coffee.

Hank nodded. "Conrad and Ethel Pool."

"You're Hank Pool?" asked Dan and Belinda in unison, noticeably shocked.

Hank laughed. "Yes."

"You don't look like the Hank we once knew," commented Dan.

Hank looked down and rubbed this thumb around the edge of his juice glass. He then looked up. "God is changing me. I do wear my hair differently and grew this beard, but mostly the change is on the inside. When I asked Jesus Christ into my heart, He gave me a new heart and a new life. He calls this process being born again. I'm a new creation; old things have passed away and all things have become new. Like Nicodemus in New Testament times, I wondered how I could be born again when I was old. The Word has shown me I'm a spirit being; I have a soul and live in a body."

"I think I hear that scripture, but do I really listen to what it's saying?" pondered Dan. "Reading the Bible after your ministry here, Hank, is like reading a new book. I was complacent and in a rut. Drinking the Lord's refreshing water has caused me to wake up. There's a stirring in my heart once again. The Holy Spirit has renewed my first love, who is Jesus Christ. Instead of just reading the Word, I've asked for the Word to read me. The Word is definitely alive!"

"That's good, Dad," agreed Joshua. "You've pinpointed an area in my life too. Sometimes I read the Word, but just kind of skim over it. I need to meditate and ask the Holy Spirit to purge my heart with His words. Waiting on the Lord and spending more time with Him will be my number one priority."

"I'm finding, too," added Belinda, "that I need to trust the Lord with every circumstance I'm faced with. We need more

CHAPTER SEVENTEEN

teaching on these areas. How long will you be staying at your parents place, Hank?"

"I don't know. However, the Lord has been showing me He'll be sending me a couple that will need deliverance. So I'll continue to wait upon Him for direction. Today though, Joshua and I are going riding. Would you mind if I borrowed a horse from you?"

Surprised, Dan and Belinda stared at each other, wondering if the couple could be Peter and Stacey.

"You can use Brandy," offered Belinda. "I think she would be all right, don't you Joshua?"

"Yes, she will be a good mount for Hank. I'm going to ride Blaze. He's really feeling his oats, so it'll be an interesting ride. He hasn't been ridden for quite some time."

"Is he new?" asked Belinda.

"I bought him for Madison. He was her birthday present."

"Did she get a chance to ride him?"

"No. We were going to go riding, but . . ." Joshua paused before continuing. "We didn't get around to it. Mom, I think this horse has potential for barrel racing. May be you could look after him when I go to Canada, and you could train him."

Belinda could see it was still difficult for Joshua to talk about Madison. She just wanted to hug all his hurt away, but she knew only the Lord could heal his broken heart. "Sure Joshua, I'd love to see what Blaze could do. When are you leaving for Canada?"

"I'm not sure yet, but I'll stay around until Hank leaves."

Just then the phone rang and Dan got up to answer it. "Hello."

"Hi, Dan."

"Pete, I'm glad you called back. We were wondering if you and your family would come for a visit. We haven't seen Emily yet."

"You don't have to convince me," replied Peter. "We've booked tickets and we're coming next weekend. We need to talk to you about this Hank Hurley."

"Okay, shall we pick you up at the airport?"

"No, we'll be renting a car. Dan, don't worry about Belinda; she'll be okay once we've had a chance to pray for her."

Dan wondered how he should reply. He mouthed for everyone to pray.

"Dan, are you still there?"

"Sorry Peter, I'm still here. Belinda and I

CHAPTER SEVENTEEN

want to talk to you both about her deliverance as well."

"We can't call it a deliverance until we check Belinda out, Dan. We'll be praying for you both. See you next Saturday."

Dan put the phone down and joined everyone at the table. They lifted their heads and looked at Dan.

"What was that all about, Dad? Are Uncle Peter and Aunt Stacey coming here?"

Dan nodded. "I'm not so sure what they're up to, but they're quite adamant about helping you, Belinda."

"So, they don't think I was delivered, do they?"

"I guess not. They're coming to pray for you. Stacey was very agitated on the phone this morning."

Hank shut his eyes and bowed his head. "*Yes, Father,*" he said quietly.

Hank looked up and spoke softly, "This is the couple I'm supposed to wait for. The Lord is preparing their hearts to receive as we speak. Stacey needs to be set free from the spirit of religion and control. She's had a very strict upbringing by her dad who is a pastor. The rules and regulations while growing up in that home have caused rebellion and opened a door for hardness to enter her heart. She has a form of godliness, but denies the power of the Lord. Stacey says all the right things, but her heart isn't open to things of the Lord. When she's released from these spirits, she'll become sweet and soft. Peter, on the other hand, needs to be the head of his home. He allows Stacey to take this position because he's afraid of her. God's pattern for the home is for the man to be head of his household. His order is to protect the family from spiritual predators."

Dan, Belinda and Joshua listened in awe. Everything Hank spoke was true. Only God and the immediate family knew about these things.

Dan broke the silence. "You're absolutely right, Hank. But I must warn you, they . . ."

Hank put up his hand to silence Dan. "Please don't tell me what they said. If the Lord wants to bring it to light, He will tell me. If not, then I would rather not know."

Dan nodded and kept what he was going to say to himself.

Hank spoke again. "I'd appreciate it if you would give yourselves to prayer. Please don't share this with anyone else. The Lord will bring those to the church who need to

CHAPTER SEVENTEEN

be there." Hank turned to Joshua, "Let's go riding!"

Joshua stood up. "I'll bring Brandy back in a day or so."

"Keep her as long as Hank stays, Joshua. I won't be riding right now as I need to do a few things around this house if we're having company next week."

"Okay Mom, thanks. I'll bring both horses back after Hank leaves."

CHAPTER EIGHTEEN

Hearing someone knocking at the front door, Belinda opened it to find Peter, Stacey and a red-faced, screaming baby. Peter and Stacey looked totally flustered. Belinda reached out and took Emily from Stacey who gave her up quickly. To their surprise, as soon as the baby was out of Stacey's arms and into Belinda's, Emily stopped crying.

"Now look at that," said Peter. "She's never done that before."

"Please come in!" invited Belinda, as she showed them into the living room. Belinda sat in the armchair leaving the sofa for Peter and Stacey. Belinda looked down at Emily, "What a beautiful little girl you are!"

Peter and Stacey sat wearily on the sofa and looked at Belinda in wonder. How did she do that?

WHEN TWO WORLDS COLLIDE

"You're not going to believe this, but she's been crying since we left home. The passengers on our flight were ready to toss us out. We couldn't get her to settle down, and now look at her." Peter sighed and continued, "She's been such a handful. We thought at first it was colic, but the doctor couldn't find anything wrong with her. Anyway, thanks for the break! It's nice to see you Belinda. Where's Dan?"

"Go on out to the barn Peter, you'll probably find him there."

Peter glanced at Stacey who gave him a slight nod and Peter escaped quickly.

Belinda watched the exchange between them and remembered what Hank had said. Looking at Stacey, she could see the distress and anxiousness holding Stacey in bondage. Belinda thought about the wonderful release Stacey could expect after being delivered and then giving the Lord full control of her life. Emily felt heavy so she looked down at her and found her sound asleep. She carefully laid her on the sofa beside Stacey, not wanting to awaken her. They put some pillows around her and tiptoed into the kitchen.

"Do you want some coffee, Stacey?"

"No thanks Belinda, but what I could use is a nap. Would you mind?"

CHAPTER EIGHTEEN

"That's a good idea, Stacey. You should get some sleep while Emily is sleeping. I've fixed Joshua's room for you and Peter."

Belinda showed her where the room was and watched as Stacey laid down and closed her eyes. Belinda shut the door quietly and went to check on the baby. She was still sleeping soundly. *"Oh Father, she's so perfect. Whatever is wrong with Emily, I ask You to heal her. Thank you in advance for Peter and Stacey's freedom!"*

Peter found Dan working on a piece of machinery. Dan wiped the grease from his hands and shook Peter's hand. He then pulled Peter toward himself and hugged him briefly.

"Sure is great seeing you again little brother. How've you been?"

Peter sighed heavily. "I'm not sure. For one thing, I'm exhausted! Emily has been so fussy and our hours of sleep are limited. We've taken her to the doctor, but he can't find anything wrong with her. I'm not sure what we'll do."

"You can give her to us," said Dan jokingly.

"That's the best offer I've had in a long time. I was seriously thinking of asking you and Belinda to take Emily for a few days so Stacey and I could have a break. Our relationship is very strained. I've tried to be patient, but I don't know if I can take much more of this."

"That bad, Peter?"

"Yes, it really is."

"I'll talk to Belinda, we'll work something out."

"I'd appreciate it Dan. By the way, how are you and Belinda doing?"

Dan smiled. "We're doing great. The Lord has restored our marriage. We're both experiencing a closer walk with Jesus. I'm looking forward to taking you and your family to church tomorrow. Some wonderful things are happening there."

Peter listened with envy in his heart. How he longed for the close relationship he once had with the Lord. Something was missing in his life.

"Stacey and I are looking forward to meeting your church family and spending time with you."

Emily started fussing in church, so Stacey was about to get up and take her out.

CHAPTER EIGHTEEN

Belinda reached for the baby instead and Emily eagerly went to her. She was soon fast asleep on her lap. Stacey looked on with envy. How did Belinda calm her down so quickly? Why was Emily always so fussy with her? Suddenly Stacey felt angry and agitated. She tried to listen to the pastor, but something stirring inside caused bitterness to rise up. Stacey thought about her dad and cringed. She had always wanted to please him, but never could. Her heart started to race, and she felt suffocated. Stacey tried standing, but it was like she was glued to the pew. A moan escaped from her mouth. What was happening to her?

Hank Hurley quickly moved toward the moan as the congregation began to worship. Peter stood, frightened by the noise coming from his wife. She was almost snarling and the look of hatred caused him to step away from her. He had seen the look once before when he hadn't been home on time to help with Emily. *"Oh God, please help her!"* It was then he noticed a man bending over her and rebuking the evil within. His long hair covered his face, but the authority in his voice made Peter tremble. Who was this guy? Where did he come from? Peter looked for Dan, but Dan was on his knees, arms lifted high, with his eyes closed. Something within Peter caused him to begin to look to heaven. *"Oh God, please forgive me! Please help us!"*

    The voice started quietly until the singer gained more confidence and allowed the Holy Spirit to sing. Joshua opened his eyes, looking for the singer. Was Madison able to join the service? It did sound like the song given to her during his mom's deliverance. No it wasn't Madison, it was his mom. He didn't know she could sing like that. Watching his aunt Stacey, he could see the transformation take place. Instead of agitation, her face now glowed with peace. Aunt Stacey was free! The congregation moved from prayer to praise. People were leaving their seats to dance and wave their arms to the Lord. Oh the glories of heaven! How could a human soul take much more? Joshua was then caught up in the joy and he felt like he could fly.

    Peter wanted to open his eyes, but his eyelids felt so heavy. He had slumped to the floor and wondered what people would think. Why should he care? All his cares seemed miles away as he felt cradled in his Father's arms. A new revelation of God's love flowed into every part of his

CHAPTER EIGHTEEN

being. Yes, love does cover a multitude of sins. *"Father, I love you. Forgive me for letting go of You and walking in my own ways. I surrender my heart to You; I desire to do those things that please You. I take back the authority You gave me for my family. Please give me an understanding heart. I need You!"*

Stacey tried to move away from His arms, but Father God held her close. ***"Do not fear My beloved daughter. I will not leave you. You can trust Me, for My plans for you are good and not evil. I demand nothing from you. I will show you how to love. My love for you never diminishes. It's not because of what you do, that I love you, it's who you are. You are My beloved child, a new creation. Because you are in My Son, you are in Me. Rest now in My love."***

Stacey heard herself sobbing, but could do nothing to stop it. She basked in the light of His Presence. A fire seemed to burn in her heart as she felt each anxiety melt away. *"Yes, I desire You, Father. I need Your love."* She didn't know if she spoke the words out loud, but she sensed the Lord was pleased with her response.

The Holy Spirit brought the congregation back to focus their attention on Pastor Blair. He now stood at the podium still experiencing the powerful move of the Holy Spirit. "God is here. As we follow and obey Him, He said He would open the gates of heaven. He did this very thing this morning. We've had deliverance, words of knowledge, tongues and interpretation of tongues. The Holy Spirit gives gifts and utterances as He wills. I believe, as we stay surrendered to the Holy Spirit, there will be much more to come. This morning we've had but a taste of what He can and is willing to do."

The congregation was dismissed, but no one wanted to move. Peter was still out under the power of God. Stacey finally made it back to her seat beside Belinda. She reached out and took Emily, who started crying at first, but once in her mother's arms she grew quiet and was content to sit with her. Stacey let the wells of water in her eyes flood her face once again. Those evil spirits had affected her daughter, too. Stacey hugged her close. It would be different now.

Peter slowly got up and sat down beside his wife. He felt wobbly and still trembled. Peter wanted to meet the man who ministered with such authority and power. He wanted to thank him.

Just then Joshua brought Hank over to

CHAPTER EIGHTEEN

meet with his aunt and uncle. "I would like you both to meet Hank Hurley."

Their eyes widened in disbelief. It couldn't be, could it? This was Hank Hurley? What about all the things they heard? *"Oh God, forgive us!"*

Stacey handed Emily back to Belinda and stood beside Peter. Peter took Hank's outstretched hand. "Thank you so much for ministering to us. It's a pleasure to meet you."

Stacey put her arms around Hank and hugged him. "Please forgive me, I've had so many horrible thoughts about you. I've accused you and didn't even know you."

Hank smiled. "I forgive you. Evil beings don't like us. They know their time here on earth is short. They'll do anything they can to keep us in fear and ignorance. We have the power and authority in Christ Jesus to command them to depart. As you continue to wait and be strengthened by the Holy Spirit, He will show you how to extract these beings from those you encounter. They will flee from you in terror. They're afraid of you because you are in Christ. You're covered by His blood and no evil can touch you."

"Please forgive me too, Hank. I want to be the man God called me to be."

WHEN TWO WORLDS COLLIDE

"I forgive you, Peter. God has given you spiritual authority to be head of your home. This is not your wife's position. You must read His word and spend time with the Lord. He has many things for you to do." Hank took Stacey's hand and put it into Peter's hand. "You're to help each other, pray for each other and submit to the Christ in each other. You both lost sight of your marriage vows. The Lord wants you to love each other as He loves you."

Peter pulled Stacey into his arms. "Please forgive me for abdicating my position, Stacey. I want our marriage to work so I recommit myself to you."

"And please forgive me for taking your spiritual headship. I was afraid if I let go of my control, you would leave me. I've been bitter and contentious. I'm so sorry Peter."

As they held each other, Hank spoke over them, "The evil one will not leave you alone just because you spoke these words over each other. You must take a stand against him and not allow him to deceive you. Keep your eyes fixed upon Jesus; He is the Author and Finisher of your faith. Remember who you are in Christ and keep forgiveness flowing to each other and those outside your home. If you don't forgive, neither can your

CHAPTER EIGHTEEN

Heavenly Father forgive you. Not forgiving can leave an open door to evil beings, so don't give them a foothold. Allowing Christ to keep your hearts pure and clean will keep you close to the Father. We can do nothing of ourselves, but we can do all things through Christ who gives us His strength."

CHAPTER NINETEEN

"**D**idn't Hank want to join us for dinner?" asked Belinda, mashing the potatoes.

"No, he couldn't. He wanted to spend some time with his parents. I think he'll be leaving soon." Joshua poured water into the glasses and then leaned against the counter. "Speaking of leaving, I'll be going to Canada next week. I'm not sure how long I'll be staying, but I'll be with the Shrivers for a couple of weeks. During that time I'll be accompanying them to the Mission in Mexico. I guess it's just across the border from San Diego."

Belinda's heart began to race, so she asked God for His peace. It came almost immediately. She looked up from the pot of potatoes and smiled at Joshua. "I know you need to do this Joshua, I just didn't think it would be so soon. Letting you go is a difficult thing for me to do, but with God's help I know I can do it."

Joshua grinned, reached over and gave her a hug. "I'll be okay, Mom. The Lord has called me and He will look after me."

"It'll be an adventure for sure Josh. Dad and I will be praying. Could you please call everyone to the table? Dinner is ready."

Dan said the blessing and everyone began passing around the platters of food.

"I wish you would have called me, Belinda. I could've given you a hand."

"That's all right, Stacey, you were busy with Emily. Joshua helped me."

Stacey looked at Joshua. "I overheard you talking to your mom, did you say you were going to Canada?"

"Yes. I'm going to meet my sisters."

"Sisters?" asked Peter, puzzled by the statement.

"Last year, just after Clara passed away, Mom and Dad received a call from a Roberta Cleveland. She was dying and needed to let Mom know her baby really did die. Remember the scam the doctor and nurses tried to hide? Well, Roberta, who was nursing then, found me and hid me for a few months. She called Grandma Harding and told her Mom's baby had

CHAPTER NINTEEN

lived. She didn't want to track down the real parents, so she let Mom believe I was her child. Roberta became a Christian before she got sick and she felt the Lord wanted her to share her story. Shortly after she shared the truth with Mom and Dad, she passed away." Joshua took a sip of water and continued, "She wrote me a letter and asked me to forgive her. She contacted the Shrivers in Cochrane and they were eager to meet with me. So, now I feel the time is right and I'd like to get to know them. Because I'm going away for an extended period of time, I was wondering if you guys would like to rent my place?" asked Joshua, directing his question to Peter and Stacey.

Peter looked at Stacey, unable to believe the timing. "Actually," said Peter, "we were going to start looking for places to rent around here. I didn't want to say anything before, but I've given up my practice in Arizona. We need a fresh start and we've always wanted to live in Montana."

"Really, guys?" grinned Dan, excited at the prospect of having his only brother closer.

"So you wouldn't mind then, if we rented Joshua's place?"

Belinda spoke up. "Peter, I think it would be wonderful! It'll be nice to get to know you both. And I'll get to watch Emily grow up."

Stacey hadn't been listening to the conversation; she was caught up in Joshua's revelation. If Joshua wasn't Belinda's son . . . then insisting Joshua know who his real father was unprecedented. Her heart burned with conviction. She had to ask Belinda to forgive her. Stacey felt all eyes on her.

"Did you hear me, Stacey?" asked Peter.

"No. I'm sorry I wasn't listening. I was thinking about Joshua's story." She then looked at Belinda. "Will you ever forgive me? I was so wrong in my judgments and the way I treated you."

"Stacey, I have forgiven you. You spoke truth in so many areas but your harshness did bother me back then. I bristled inside when you came near me. But I see through my own journey, how we all need to walk in forgiveness and repentance. I was very strong-willed and Dan can attest to that!"

Dan laughed. "That's my girl, full of spitfire, and never a dull moment!"

Everyone joined Dan in the laughter, including Belinda.

CHAPTER NINTEEN

"So, what was the question, Peter?" asked Stacey.

"Would you like to stay with Belinda and Dan while I tie a few loose ends up at home?"

"Are you sure you'd like to tackle that by yourself?"

Peter nodded. He didn't want to let on he needed some time alone.

"Yes, Emily and I would like that very much!"

Joshua pushed himself away from the table and stood up. "I've some things to settle, too. Thanks for dinner Mom; it was really good. Uncle Peter, I'll give you a call later. We'll need to go over some things about the place. Mom, I'll bring Brandy and Blaze over tomorrow."

"Dad and I would like to take you to the airport, Joshua."

"I was counting on that, Mom. I've booked the flight for next Wednesday. It's 10:30 a.m. so I should be there a couple of hours ahead of time."

Belinda's heart felt heavy but she kept a smile on her face. "We'll get you there on time, Josh."

Joshua put his hand on her shoulder and looked into her eyes. "You're not losing me mom. You know I have to do this."

"I know it in my head Joshua, it'll just take my heart a little longer to catch up. God has a special plan for you and I'll try not to get in the way."

Joshua bent down and kissed her cheek. After leaving the house, he began to think about the decisions he had made. He wondered if meeting with the Shrivers was such a good idea after all. Was this how Abraham, in the Old Testament, felt like . . . pulling up his tent pegs and going to a land he did not know? He knew the Lord was drawing him out of the familiar and into the unknown. He would just have to trust the Lord and keep his eyes fixed upon Him. Joshua drove to the cemetery and settled himself down beside Madison's grave. Someone had been there, for fresh flowers covered the ground. Joshua picked up one of the flowers and toyed with the petals. He knew this site only contained the shell of Madison, for in heaven she was very much alive. But just being here, he felt close to her somehow. He felt silly speaking out loud to her grave, but he sensed the need to speak his thoughts.

"Please forgive me for taking my eyes off the road for that split second, Maddie.

CHAPTER NINTEEN

I'm so sorry I didn't get you to put your seat belt on. We could've had a wonderful life together. There are so many things I didn't get a chance to tell you. I'm leaving Montana for a while. I believe the Lord is calling me to a mission in Mexico. I don't know what's in store for me there, but I want to heed His call."

Joshua stood up and placed the flower back on the heap of flowers.

"Do you think you'll come back here one day, Hank?" asked Ethel, as she folded the last shirt and handed it to him.

"Sometimes the Lord shows me ahead of time, but mostly I find myself just showing up. I'm so glad He allowed me to stay longer. I dreaded it at first, for I knew how much I hurt you both."

Ethel slipped her arm around his waist and pulled him close. "Forgiveness is so freeing. We needed forgiveness too, Hank. Being so set in our ways, I know our rebellion hurt the Lord's heart. Dad and I are so thankful for a new start and we desire to do everything pleasing to the Lord. I wish you could stay longer but I know I must let you go. You're in good hands!"

Conrad stood in the hallway just outside the room where mother and son were talking. His heart soared with praise and thanksgiving. A son who was lost and now found; how it thrilled him. Conrad now felt such a connection to the scripture, where Jesus left the ninety and nine to search out for the one who was lost. Conrad entered the room and put his hand on Hank's shoulder. *"Our son was lost but now he is found. Thank you Father, for bringing him back to us. Even though we know he can't stay with us, he will always be in our hearts. We give him back to You Father, for we know he is safe with You."*

Tears glistened in Hank's eyes as he put his arms around them both.

Joan and Edward sat across the table from Joshua and listened as he poured out his heart to them.

"I'm trying to be still, to wait upon God and listen to His call, but it's difficult. I'm uneasy about moving to another country."

CHAPTER NINTEEN

Joshua stirred his coffee and looked up to find Joan and Edward staring at him intently.

"We thought you and Maddie would be raising your children here but the Lord definitely had other plans, Joshua. He took Madison and now He is taking you to another place too. We'll try not to question, but it's hard. Change is always difficult but like you have taught us, if we keep our eyes focused upon Jesus, He will always lead and guide us," stated Edward.

"Prayer will keep us close to one another," added Joan. "I miss Madison terribly, but knowing she is safe in our Heavenly Father's arms heals this hole in our hearts." Joan's tears slipped down her cheeks.

Edward put his arm around Joan's shoulder and sighed heavily. "The pain of losing a child is so severe at times but each day we try to give this hurt back to God. He knows what we're going through."

"Can we pray?" whispered Joshua.

Edward and Joan nodded and bowed their heads along with him.

CHAPTER TWENTY

"Mom, Mom!" called Joshua, as he neared the house.

Belinda met him at the door with her finger to her lips, "Shhh, you'll wake up Emily. What's wrong?"

"There's been a change of plans," said Joshua lowering his voice. "I'm supposed to meet Doug and Cynthia in San Diego. Something has happened at the Mission and they're going early. Can you take me to the airport this afternoon?"

"I'm sorry Joshua, Stacey went shopping and I don't expect her back until this evening. May be Dad can take you."

"No, he can't either. He and Tyler are gone for the day. I'll give Edward and Joan a call; may be they can give me a lift."

After speaking to Edward, Joshua sat down at the kitchen table. "They'll be over in a few minutes. Mom, here are the keys for Uncle Peter. Can you make sure you also give him this list I've made up for him?"

"Yes, I'll look after it for you," assured Belinda. "I guess my dinner party for you will have to wait until you come back."

"Oh yeah. Sorry Mom. You can still have it, I just won't be there."

Belinda smiled. "It's hard to have a party when the guest of honor isn't here. Instead of a going away party, I'll have a homecoming party."

Just then Edward and Joan drove into the yard. "I have to go Mom. I'll call you and let you know what's happening. Say goodbye to Dad for me and remember we're only a prayer away."

Tears collected in Belinda's eyes as she hugged Joshua and then let him go. "I'll be praying every day for you."

"Thanks, Mom. I'll see you later." Joshua picked up his bags and hurried not wanting to keep his ride waiting.

Belinda watched until the Lindens' truck left the yard. She sat down at the kitchen table and let new tears roll down her cheeks. If she wasn't losing her son, why did she feel like her heart was breaking? Why did this goodbye seem so final? Belinda closed her

CHAPTER TWENTY

eyes and lifted her head. *"Father, I need You. I need You to ease this ache in my heart. I need You to look after Joshua and bring him home safely. Please give me Your strength so I can trust You with Joshua."*

After the plane touched down in San Diego, Joshua headed towards the baggage carousel. Excitement arose in his heart. He felt the Lord's Presence as he stood waiting for his luggage to appear. Just then someone tapped him on the shoulder. He turned around to find Doug and Cynthia smiling at him.

"Joshua, hello," beamed Cynthia, greeting him with a hug.

Doug held out his hand and Joshua, after moving away from Cynthia, gripped it.

"Did you have a good flight?" asked Doug.

"Yes. Not much room for the legs but it was smooth."

"As soon as we get your bags, we'll fill you in on all the events at the Mission," said Doug.

Joshua noticed his duffle bags and reached out to put them next to him.

WHEN TWO WORLDS COLLIDE

"That's all I have," he said, hoisting one on his shoulder and picking up the other one.

"My," said Cynthia, "you sure travel light."

Joshua smiled. "I didn't really know what to bring, so if I need anything, I'll just get it here."

"Good idea, Joshua," agreed Doug. "Let's go."

The Shrivers had rented a utility vehicle with four-wheel drive. Joshua was puzzled about their choice. The Mission was supposedly in the city of Tijuana, not in a rural location.

"We're not going to the Mission right now, Joshua," said Doug, as if he read his mind. "There's a young woman in serious trouble and we're going to find her and take her to the Mission. She's been hiding out in a little town outside of the city and we'll need this vehicle for the roads, which are quite rugged. We've been in touch with her before. She's recently come to know Jesus as her personal Savior, and she's in danger because she refuses to go back to her previous lifestyle. Her boss is very angry and wants her back."

Joshua listened, his heart racing with excitement once again. "So how, then, is the Mission involved with her?"

CHAPTER TWENTY

"She received Christ through their ministry. I guess she fled there when being pursued by the drug dealers," replied Doug.

"Drug dealers? She's involved with drugs?"

"No, I don't think she's a user. She just delivered them."

"So why doesn't she go to the police, then?"

Doug found a street to turn off and parked the vehicle. He turned around and faced Joshua. "Joshua, this is a dangerous ordeal because the police are involved. Her father is one of the constables and also a dealer. When we cross the border you mustn't speak. Cynthia knows some Spanish and will do the talking. Do you know any Spanish?"

"A little, just what I learned in school."

"Well, keep it to yourself. The reason Martha called us is because foreigners may have a slight advantage where this case is concerned. We may have to barter for her life if we're caught trying to take her across the border."

"She's not staying at the Mission?"

"No. We think she'll be safer in Canada. She has agreed to live with us in Cochrane."

"Does this girl have a name?"

Cynthia answered, "Her name is Angelina."

Joshua took a deep breath. "Well, we better go get Angelina then."

Doug pulled the vehicle back into traffic and drove towards the border. At the border a uniformed man waved them on.

"That's amazing," exclaimed Cynthia. "I think it's the first time we've gone through without being stopped. It can be quite frustrating when they tear your vehicle apart."

"This will be the easy part of the plan, crossing the border. We still have several miles to travel and we've been told it's not wise to drive at night. I believe the Lord can go ahead and make all the crooked places straight," commented Doug.

He turned off the freeway and almost immediately they experienced rough roads. The holes in some spots seemed like crevices and Doug tried to maneuver around them. The truck bounced along the road, jarring the passengers. Joshua closed his eyes at one point and asked the Lord for safety. It was dusk when they arrived at the town. No roads seemed to lead into the place so Doug tried to dodge trees and

CHAPTER TWENTY

large rocks. He finally could go no further, so parked the vehicle by a grove of trees.

"Cynthia, you stay here while Joshua and I go and get Angelina. If there's any trouble, drive back to the Mission and we'll meet you there."

"Okay, Doug. God go with you and keep you safe."

Doug motioned for Joshua to follow him.

Joshua caught up to Doug and whispered, "You mean to tell me, Cynthia knows how to get back to the Mission from here?"

"We've had these rescues before, Joshua. God has given her directions and she has always found her way back to the Mission."

Joshua found this quite amazing. He wondered what God had in store. Would they be able to rescue Angelina and make it back to Canada? Only time would tell.

They soon found themselves in front of a small shack and Doug knocked on the door. A small dog yapped at them as it came around the side of the house. A woman appeared at the door and beckoned them inside. Joshua tried to adjust his eyes but as dark as it was outside, it was just as dark inside. The woman then lit a small candle and large shadows loomed on the walls. The small shack had one bed, a wooden box for a table, and what looked like a sink, but Joshua thought it had to be a washtub. On the bed, four children and a young woman sat cross-legged.

"Angelina is ready," said the woman in broken English.

The young woman, hearing her name, came to the woman's side. The woman put her arm around the young woman's shoulder and she winced.

Without thinking about her guests being men, the older woman peeled back the young woman's blouse to reveal her pain. The skin was broken and caked with blood. The woman took a concoction from near her sink and stroked the young woman's shoulder with it. She spoke softly in Spanish and the girl's eyes filled with tears. She nodded and hugged her.

Doug and Joshua looked on with sympathy. How did her shoulder receive such a blow? The girl looked blankly at Doug and Joshua as she went towards them. Doug thanked the woman and motioned the girl to follow them. Once in the truck, Cynthia sat in the back with Angelina and spoke

CHAPTER TWENTY

softly to her in Spanish. This seemed to ease her fears and she laid her head on Cynthia's lap. Angelina was soon asleep.

CHAPTER TWENTY-ONE

Several miles over rough terrain, and in the early morning hour, Joshua woke up as Doug pulled in front of an iron gate. He honked once and a small woman with grey hair opened the gate for them. They drove up into what looked like a courtyard. The truck was soon surrounded with young faces peering in the windows. A young boy opened Joshua's door and pulled at him to join him. Doug, Cynthia and Angelina had already vacated the vehicle and were in deep conversation with the grey-haired woman. Every once in awhile she would lift her head and look intently his way. The little boy put his hand in Joshua's and led him into a large room. Joshua looked around and realized, after seeing the tables and benches, that he was in the dining area. The little boy had retrieved Joshua a steaming cup of brew

WHEN TWO WORLDS COLLIDE

and he gratefully sat down at one of the tables.

"So this is where you are, Manuel. You go get your books and be ready for school," ordered a young woman in Spanish.

Joshua watched as the boy quickly obeyed. He flashed Joshua a huge smile and waved at him.

Joshua waved back. The young woman sat across from Joshua and extended her hand to him. "I'm Sarita, Martha's daughter."

"Joshua, my name's Joshua Cole."

Sarita smiled, "I like your name. It's from the Bible, right?"

"You speak English quite well."

"Thanks, I used to live in the States." Sarita glanced down at the watch around her neck. "I'll see you later Joshua. I have to walk the little ones to school."

Joshua looked down at his cup and wondered if it would be safe to drink it. He had heard once how the water in Mexico did strange things to your stomach. As he was thinking this, Doug came over and sat down beside him.

"I see you've met Sarita. And you can drink your coffee, they use pure water here."

CHAPTER TWENTY-ONE

Joshua put the cup to his lips and found the liquid quite satisfying. "Yes, she seems nice. The little boy who pulled me out of the truck . . . is he an orphan?"

"Manuel? Yes, he's an orphan. Most of the children here have parents but they are very poor and can't afford to feed them, let alone send them to school. This mission looks after their children. On school holidays and some weekends they go to their own homes so they can visit their families. But Manuel came here as a baby and the Mission is his home."

"So where are Angelina and Cynthia?"

"They're getting ready for the wedding."

"Angelina is getting married?" asked Joshua, stunned by Doug's nonchalant statement.

"Yes, she is Joshua, and you will be the groom."

Joshua stared back at Doug in disbelief. "You're kidding, right?"

"No, Joshua. We've thought this through and the only way Angelina can freely go to the United States is by being married to an American."

Joshua's heart started to race. "You knew about this before I met you in San Diego?"

"I'm sorry Joshua, we couldn't let you in on it there. We were afraid you wouldn't come."

"Listen Doug, marriage is very sacred to me. I can't marry someone I don't love."

Doug paused before laying out his case. "As soon as we get Angelina out of Mexico, you can have the marriage annulled in San Diego. It's just that simple."

Joshua looked at this man who was supposed to be his biological father. What a horrible thing to do to someone. This was insane! And simple? Had the man gone totally mad?

"So, what do you say, can we count you in?"

Joshua shook his head. "I'm not marrying someone I don't know, Doug. You'll have to think of another plan."

"Okay Joshua, but could you please pray about this? I'll take you to where you'll be sleeping and you can spend some time with the Lord."

I could spend three weeks alone with the Lord and come up with the same answer, thought Joshua to himself as he followed Doug. Joshua let his body sag as he sat on the edge of the cot. *"Oh God, tell me this isn't happening. Is this Your plan for my*

CHAPTER TWENTY-ONE

life? I came here to help, but marriage wasn't part of the plan, was it? What about Madison? My heart belongs to her! I don't know this girl Father. How can I marry her?"

"Let go, Joshua, and be still. I have made a way where there is no way. I open doors, which no man can shut, and I close doors, which no man can open. Trust Me, Joshua. I will be with you."

Joshua knew the voice of his Father, but somehow these words didn't ease the anxiety he felt in his heart. He had been set up! Anger surfaced in his heart. How could Doug and Cynthia use him like this? Had their wanting to get to know him been only a ploy? Joshua felt sick to his stomach. He was in a different country and didn't even know how to speak the language. He felt alone even though the Lord had just said He would not leave him alone. He must speak with his mom and dad before he decided anything. Joshua found Doug in the kitchen, laughing with the cook. Joshua was not amused.

"Hey, Joshua, did you hear from the Lord yet?"

"I'd like to give Mom and Dad a call before any decision is made."

Doug stopped smiling and looked intently at Joshua. "I'm sorry, son, but the phone may be tapped and we can't take that chance." Doug reached out to put his hand on Joshua's shoulder.

Joshua pulled back like he had been burned. "I'm not your son, Doug, please don't call me that again." Joshua turned on his heel and left the kitchen.

Cynthia joined Doug and watched Joshua leave the room. "Doug, I don't have good feeling about this anymore. I thought we heard from the Lord, but maybe we were wrong."

"He'll see this our way, Cynthia. We did hear from the Lord because it was confirmed by three different sources. We must be patient and wait. I know Joshua listens to the Lord and he will be obedient to whatever the Lord shows him to do. Now, where is Angelina?"

"She's gone shopping with Martha. Angelina is using money she received from her father, so they're looking for a wedding gown. She wants the wedding to be extravagant so word can be spread quickly about her marriage."

"Is that safe?"

"Martha says not to worry; evil only comes out at night."

Doug put his arm around Cynthia and

CHAPTER TWENTY-ONE

hugged her. "Everything will be all right. If God is for us, who can be against us?"

Cynthia looked up at her husband and smiled. Anxious thoughts could not crowd her mind; she had to be still and know that God had everything in His hands.

Back in his room, Joshua looked out of the small window. So many feelings caused tightness in his chest. At one point he just wanted to scream obscenities at Doug and Cynthia for getting him into this mess in the first place. Then total betrayal was the next feeling. How could he not be able to call his mom and dad? If the Mission was a safe place, how could the lines be tapped? How could Doug and Cynthia let this happen? Joshua's heart burned. He needed peace and there was only one place he knew where this peace existed. Joshua knelt beside the cot and looked heavenward. *"I can't seem to talk to anyone but You, Father. I know You have called me and anointed me for Your work. If this is my mission, then I'll gladly do what You would have me do. I don't understand this leading but I surrender my feelings to You. Please forgive me for being angry with Doug. I know man's anger does not promote the righteousness of God, so I will not give this anger a foothold in my heart. I will ask Doug to forgive me before this day is over. I will keep my eyes fixed upon You, for You are the Author and Finisher of my faith. I worship You Father!"*

Even before he finished his last words to his Heavenly Father, peace covered him like a blanket. His testing was to be still and wait upon the Lord. These words sent shivers into his soul. He ministered these very words to the congregation and now he would have to live them. Joshua heard the Word speaking to him. ***"My brethren, count it all joy when you fall into various trials, knowing that the testing of your faith produces patience. But let patience have its perfect work, that you may be perfect and complete, lacking nothing. If any of you lacks wisdom, let him ask of God, who gives to all liberally and without reproach, and it will be given to him."*** [10]

[10] James 1:1-5

CHAPTER TWENTY-TWO

Joshua could hardly breathe as he watched Angelina walk down the church aisle towards him. Where was the young girl he had met in the tiny shack? The girl approaching him was a woman . . . a beautiful woman. She was petite with long silky black hair. Her dress was white satin and shimmered as she walked. Soon she stood beside him and looked shyly up at him. Her appearance overwhelmed him and he knew he looked foolish staring at her. He reached down and took her hand in his. She was trembling. Joshua squeezed her hand to reassure her it was going to be all right. He didn't understand what the minister was saying, but on cue he remembered to say 'I do'. A supper was being held in their honor at a fancy hotel in Tijuana. Angelina Morales Cortez was married and soon everyone would know. Her father no longer had any jurisdiction over her. She was married to an American and could freely enter into the United States.

"Angelina is a smart girl," sneered Constable Cortez. "She'll run for us between countries. I've taught her well. No matter she didn't invite me to the wedding; it's better this way. I'll have a little chat with her husband before she leaves. He will understand what is expected of him."

"I have the room number of where they're staying. I'll bring him to you," assured his aide.

"I'll be waiting for him."

Doug took Joshua aside after the dinner. "Joshua, thank you for making the wedding look so real. I know this is hard for you. We have people watching the hotel, so you will only have to spend one night here. We have purchased our tickets and will fly out of San Diego tomorrow night. We are just waiting for Angelina's papers to be processed for her passport."

"Doug, we're not going to Canada right away. I'd like Angelina to meet my mom and dad."

CHAPTER TWENTY-TWO

"What do you mean, Joshua? This is not how the plan goes. She will be safer in Canada."

"Trust me Doug, I know what I'm doing. I've already made arrangements for us to fly to Montana. You and Cynthia are welcome to join us there before you go back to Canada."

"Joshua, I don't know what you're up to, but it's too dangerous. You don't know whom you are dealing with. These are evil men and we need Angelina to be safe with us."

"I'm not budging on this, Doug. We go to Montana first."

Doug felt heat rise in his face as he glared at Joshua. What foolish prank was this? Joshua had to follow the plan. Did something already happen that he was unaware of? Did the drug runners threaten him and Angelina? For now, he would be still. But Angelina was going with him and Cynthia and that was what he knew.

"I'm taking Angelina to the room now, Doug. I'll talk to you later."

With that said, Joshua found Angelina standing with Cynthia and took her hand in his. She looked apprehensive so Joshua smiled. "Tell her we're just going to our room, Cynthia."

WHEN TWO WORLDS COLLIDE

    Cynthia looked at Doug who was seething inside. Doug just nodded and Cynthia spoke softly to Angelina who then squeezed Joshua's hand.
    Once in the room, Joshua's heart began to race. Why had he said all those things to Doug? He didn't have a different plan. Where had all those words come from? The horrified look on Angelina's face at that precise moment caused Joshua to wheel around. A large object slammed into his skull and he crumpled.

    Coming to, Joshua felt his head to find blood trickling down the side of his face. Joshua groaned and tried to sit up. A putrid smell filled his nostrils and made his eyes burn. His feet felt cold and he looked down to see his boots had been taken from him. Where was he? And more importantly, where was Angelina? His suit jacket was also missing and he felt chilled on the damp concrete floor. Suddenly a door clanged open and two uniformed men pulled him to his feet. One on each side of him, they dragged him through the door

CHAPTER TWENTY-TWO

and then Joshua heard it clang shut again. Was he in a jail? Joshua was then taken to a room with one chair. The men plopped him on it and left. Joshua looked around and shivered. He looked down and found his suit pants torn and his knees scraped. How long had he been here? What kind of hell was he in? Joshua didn't have to wait long for his answers. A man entered, also in uniform, but looking more important than the two who had escorted him in.

"Ah, Senor Cole, nice of you to pay me a visit. You hurt my feelings by not inviting me to your wedding. My daughter has good taste," said the man, leering into Joshua's face. "Let me introduce myself, I'm Luis Cortez, your new father-in-law!"

Joshua listened to his evil laughter and knew he was not in good company.

"This is the deal, Senor Cole, you're part of my family now, so you will work for me."

Joshua shook his head. "I only have one master and His name is Jesus Christ."

Luis Cortez sneered. "When my men are through with you, Senor, you'll be cursing this name!"

Angelina then burst into the room. "Please papa, I will do anything you say, but please do not injure this man."

WHEN TWO WORLDS COLLIDE

Mr. Cortez went over and put his arm around his daughter. "You're right, my sweet, you will do what I say and so will your new husband. I'm glad you're married; now we'll have better business connections in the United States. I couldn't have thought of a better plan myself. Well done, Angelina!"

Angelina tried pulling away, but her father wouldn't let her go.

"Let Joshua go and I'll continue to work for you."

"I make the deals, Angelina," he sneered. "And it made me very angry when you ran away. Don't be thinking about doing that again. I won't be lenient with you a second time."

Joshua stared at Angelina; her English was perfect. What else could she be keeping from him? But then again, he didn't know her at all. *"Father, I need Your help! Please show me what to do."*

As Joshua sat there, a supernatural strength filled him. His sagging shoulders grew taut and he felt His Father's peace fill every part of his being. ***"Be still and when it is time for you to speak, I will give you the words."***

Mr. Cortez suddenly moved away from Angelina and he spit his next words at

CHAPTER TWENTY-TWO

Joshua. "She's damaged goods, Senor Cole. Did you know this before you said I do? She's been married before, and not with my permission."

"And you had him killed, Papa. I'll never forgive you! I hate you and I wish you were dead!"

"Accusations, that's all you have. Where's your proof? He was one of my men. Why would I have him killed? Enough, I have work to do! I've fixed up a room for the two of you and you will wait there until I send for you. Again, Joshua, welcome to my family!"

A uniformed man entered and escorted them to the new room. They entered and then heard the door being locked behind them.

Angelina threw herself down on the bed and wept.

Joshua surveyed the room and then sat on the edge of the bed. He was no longer in the dreadful cell and felt tremdous relief.

"You've been married before?"

Angelina slowly sat up and looked at Joshua. Tears glistened in her eyes and she whispered, "I'm so sorry it's turned out this way. No, I was not married before. I will explain later. We were to have this marriage annulled in San Diego and go our separate ways. I never wanted to be married; my heart belongs to Anton. My father is a cruel man, so you'll have to be cautious. I don't know how we can escape."

As Joshua listened to her, his heart ached, wondering what kind of life she had had to endure. "We must stay focused on Jesus, Angelina. Our escape will be through Him. I've recently lost my fiancée, so I had no intention of being married either. We will wait upon the Lord and listen for His instructions. I sense we need to get a message to Martha. Is this possible?"

"If Papa still has Hermosa working as the cook, we can trust her. She's a Christian. I know she'll be able to get a message to Martha."

"I'm kind of hungry. Can we send for her now?"

Angelina smiled. She walked over and picked up the phone on the desk. She spoke rapidly in Spanish and set the phone down. "Hermosa is there and she'll be right up. She doesn't speak English so I'll explain to her what she needs to do."

"That's fine, Angelina. Just let Martha know we are fine and we will try and come to the Mission."

"Do you think we can?"

CHAPTER TWENTY-TWO

"Yes, God can make a way where there is no way."

"It seems you have a direct line to God, do you Joshua?"

"When we accept Jesus into our hearts, we all have a direct line, Angelina. We just need to have our ears trained to hear and God will direct us."

"I don't think I hear very well then Joshua. He does not speak to me like He speaks to you."

"Keep listening Angelina. You will hear," encouraged Joshua.

They heard the door unlocking and Hermosa, with a uniformed man, stepped into the room. She walked over and put the tray on the desk, the man watching her every move. Hermosa quickly reached out for Angelina and hugged her tightly before the man grabbed her arm. He roughly pulled her out of the room with him.

"Now what are we going to do? You couldn't even speak to the woman." Joshua sighed and lifted the linen cloth on the tray. His eyes lit up to find steaming cups of coffee and tortilla's filled with meat. He pulled up a chair, prayed and began to devour the food.

Angelina took her tortilla, scraped the meat onto her plate and placed a piece of paper on the tortilla. She then wrapped it up again and took a couple of bites. Angelina took her cup and slowly sipped the coffee. "We should hear back from Martha in a couple of days."

Joshua marveled at her ingenuity. He felt hope seep into his heart as he looked at her. "Angelina, you're very beautiful."

Angelina blushed. "Thank you, Joshua."

After finding some suitable clothes in the closet to wear, Joshua knelt down beside the bed. He wondered why the clothes he found fit him so well. He would have to ask Angelina about this. She was taking a bath so Joshua thought this would be a good time to spend in prayer. Joshua began to speak softly in his spirit language. He prayed for a few minutes and then sensed stillness in his soul. Joshua continued to wait silently before the Lord, his head bowed and eyes closed. Someone tapped him on the shoulder and Joshua opened his eyes. There, standing beside him, was Hank Hurley.

"Hank," whispered Joshua, not really believing what he was seeing, "it's too dangerous for you to be here."

"It's okay, Joshua. God sent me here. We don't have much time, so let's go to the Mission."

CHAPTER TWENTY-TWO

Joshua stood up beside Hank and put a hand on his shoulder. He wasn't dreaming . . . it was Hank all right! Angelina was going to be so excited. They were being rescued!

"I'll see if Angelina can get dressed quickly."

"Angelina?"

Didn't Hank know about Angelina? "My wife, Angelina, she's in the bathroom."

"You're married? When did this happen?"

"A few days ago, but I'll tell you more at the Mission." Joshua went over and knocked gently on the door.

"Just a minute Joshua, I'll be right out."

"Angelina? We have company so I'll get you something to wear."

Joshua found some clothes in another closet and opened the bathroom door slightly to pass them to her. Angelina peeked around the door. "Who's here, Joshua?"

"A friend. He's here to take us to the Mission."

"Our note would not have been delivered that quickly, Joshua. Do you know this friend?"

"Yes, now quickly . . . get dressed."

Joshua turned back into the room to find Hank sitting in the chair beside the desk.

247

"Have you thought about an escape route Hank?"

"Yes, God will open the doors for us."

"And the Lord didn't tell you about Angelina?"

"I guess I didn't need to know, Joshua. I was only told to take you to the Mission. Also I have a name of a detective in San Diego you are to contact when you arrive there. It seems they have been trying to break up this drug ring for quite some time. Every man they've sent into Mexico has never returned. They're quite pleased that you'll be able to help them."

"I don't know what I can do. I do know I'd like to see Angelina safe from this maniac who's her father. He's evil personified."

"Looks like he roughed you up a bit."

"A little, but the Lord gave me His strength through the ordeal. I was passed out most of the time, I think. I don't remember much."

"I know Joshua, I was there."

"So this is what happens on your spirit travels. You get to watch the torture of other people?"

Hank's heart ached at Joshua's perception. "I don't enjoy it, if that's what you're implying. I pray and intercede for the individual."

CHAPTER TWENTY-TWO

"Sorry, Hank, that didn't come out right. I'm glad you were there to pray for me. I'm not sure if I'm ready for Spirit travel; I just thought you went to heavenly places, not to the hellish places on earth."

"It works both ways, Joshua. I wait on the Lord and He sends me where He wants me to go. I see the evil of this world and the wonder of the heavenly world. And Joshua, you are ready for Spirit travel too. I want you to know this is found in the scriptures. When you're not a Christian this kind of travel is known as astral projection. But we are filled with the Holy Spirit and that is why I call it Spirit travel. Remember Philip in Acts chapter eight, after he had baptized the eunuch? The Spirit of the Lord caught Philip up and took him somewhere else."

Just then Angelina entered the room. She had her hair pinned up and she looked like a model that just stepped out of a catalogue. "I'm ready," she announced.

"Angelina, this is Hank Hurley. He's a friend from back home."

Angelina extended her hand to Hank. "It's a pleasure to meet you Hank. You're here to take us to the Mission?"

Hank smiled. She was beautiful. Joshua was a blessed man. "Yes, let's go."

WHEN TWO WORLDS COLLIDE

Hank led them to the door and opened it without difficulty. The guard at the door slept soundly as the three walked passed him. No one seemed to be on guard in the rest of the building, which Joshua found strange. God was making a way for them, and there was no doubting it.

CHAPTER TWENTY-THREE

The greeting they received at the Mission was a tearful one. Doug and Cynthia, having returned from San Diego could not believe their eyes when Joshua and Angelina walked into the courtyard.

"We've been so worried about you two. What happened? Where have you been for two weeks?" asked Doug, as he and Joshua sat at one of the long tables in the eating area.

"Two weeks, we've been gone that long? I don't know, but it was a pretty posh place compared to the dungeon I was originally in. I think I was in a jail cell for the first while. Then I was taken to Mr. Cortez's residence where Angelina was."

Doug looked horrified. "You escaped from the Cortez place? No one I've heard of gets out of there alive. It's so well guarded how . . . did you manage it?"

"I was amazed too, Doug. The Lord sent Hank Hurley to help us."

"And who's Hank Hurley?"

"He's just an ordinary man, but God uses him in remarkable ways. He spirit travels. Have you ever heard of such a thing?"

"Yes, but it can be dangerous if you follow the wrong spirits. I wouldn't want to try it. I want my feet firmly planted on solid ground. So, let me get this right: this Hank came from who knows where and rescued you from the Cortez place?"

"We're here, aren't we?"

"And where is Hank, then?"

"As soon as we were at the gate he left. He did give me a name though of a detective in San Diego who has been trying to break this drug ring. Hank said we could trust him with our information."

"I know Joshua, his name is Jose Armando."

"You know him too?"

"Cynthia and I have been with him for the last two days trying to figure how to get you out of the clutches of Luis Cortez. They've been watching him for some time. I'll let Jose know you have been rescued and he can take it from there. So, I want to know about this different plan you had at the wedding."

CHAPTER TWENTY-THREE

"I didn't have a different plan Doug. Guess I wanted to see how you felt about someone else rearranging your life for you."

"Please forgive me Joshua, we just couldn't see another way out for Angelina. We can also have the marriage annulled in San Diego. But Angelina is a pretty girl, isn't she?"

"No, Doug, she's beautiful. And I wouldn't call her a girl; she's definitely a woman."

Doug smiled. "No hard feelings then?"

"None. I will do whatever I can to see Angelina safely in Canada. I'm beat. Do I sleep in the same room as before?"

"Yes, and I'll see you in the morning."

As Joshua strolled through the courtyard, he could hear voices coming from Martha's office. Angelina appeared at the doorway and called out, "Joshua, can I speak to you for a moment?"

Joshua turned towards her and stopped to listen to what she had to say.

"I want to thank you very much for helping me. I feel safe with you, Joshua. You are a good man." Angelina stood up on her tiptoes to reach Joshua and kissed him on the cheek.

Something in Joshua's heart melted at that instant. He suddenly knew he could let go of Madison and be a husband to Angelina. Did she feel the same way?

Angelina waited for a reply but Joshua stood silent. Not knowing what to do, she turned and went back into Martha's office.

Cynthia came over and put her arm around Angelina. "What did he say?"

"Nothing. I waited but he didn't react one way or the other. I thought I needed to hold onto Anton, but my heart now beats for Joshua. Will God show me how to make Joshua see this?"

"If you are meant to be with one another, God will make a way," assured Cynthia. "Now you better get some sleep. Tomorrow will be a long day."

Angelina went through a door in Martha's office and found a room to sleep in. Angelina lay on her bed and spoke to her new father. *"Father, thank you for taking me out of evil. Please save my papa. He needs to be rescued by You. I'm sorry for hating him and wanting him to die. Thank you for giving me Joshua. Please show me how to be a good wife."* Angelina closed her eyes and sleep came immediately.

Joshua awoke early and noticed a bookshelf in his room. He scanned the titles and picked out an interesting title,

CHAPTER TWENTY-THREE

'Darkness Exposed . . . Passages from the Spirit'. He was glad to see it was written in English. After reading a couple of the passages, he flipped back to the first page. He noticed the author was from Cochrane. He would have to remember to ask Doug and Cynthia if they knew her. Joshua left his room and went to the eating area. Manuel was there again to greet him. He quickly brought Joshua some coffee and a plate of eggs and tortillas.

"Gracias, Manuel."

Manuel beamed and sat down beside Joshua.

Joshua looked down at his new friend. Manuel was neatly dressed in a white shirt and grey slacks. Joshua guessed this was another school day for him. With everything happening, Joshua didn't even know what day it was. Manuel reached up and grabbed Joshua's finger and tried to pry his ring off.

"Sorry buddy, but that's my wedding ring. Yeah, it's new to me too. But if I'm hearing right, it will stay there until death do us part."

Joshua didn't know whether the boy could understand or not, but he just smiled and left the ring alone.

WHEN TWO WORLDS COLLIDE

"I thought I would find you here with Joshua, Manuel. I see you are ready for school this time. Good boy," praised Sarita as she flashed a smile Joshua's way. "I've even got time for a coffee this morning. So, Joshua, I hear you got married. Kind of a sudden decision, wasn't it? Guess it was love at first sight. Angelina sure is happy!"

"She is? I mean, we're both happy," answered Joshua, stumbling, not sure what to say.

"Guess you have the marriage jitters. Where is your bride this morning? You didn't want to eat together?"

Joshua smiled. She sure asked a lot of questions. "She decided to sleep in, I guess."

Sarita took another sip from her coffee. "Come on Manuel, time for school. I see the other children are waiting for us by the gate. May be I'll see you later, Joshua?"

Joshua nodded. He didn't know what was happening today. He could be in another country, for all he knew.

Manuel hugged Joshua before he hurried off with Sarita.

"Looks like Manuel is getting quite attached to you, Joshua," said Martha as she sat across the table from him.

CHAPTER TWENTY-THREE

"He seems like a lovable little guy. How old is he?"

"He'll be eight in a couple of months. Now, why is it that you and Angelina did not share a room last night?"

Martha's question caught him totally off guard. Martha didn't know of Doug and Cynthia's plan?

"Marriage is sacred. You must take your vows seriously. Have you already had a disagreement?"

"Martha, I think you should talk to Doug and Cynthia."

"They seem to have a solid relationship, I don't think they need advice in this area. I heard Angelina crying this morning; I think you should go to her and comfort her."

Martha's look made Joshua uncomfortable and he wanted to obey. He thought he'd find Doug and get this situation cleared up. It was Doug after all, who made all the wedding arrangements.

Joshua moved away from the table and walked towards Martha's office. He knocked softly at the door and Cynthia greeted him.

"Good Morning, Cynthia. Can I please have some time with Angelina?"

"Sure Joshua, I'll get her."

Joshua could hear the women whispering before Angelina came into the office. Cynthia walked passed them and left them alone.

"Angelina . . ." started Joshua.

"Please, Joshua, let me speak first. I must tell you about myself."

They found chairs and sat down across from one another.

"Before coming to Christ, Joshua, I did many wicked things. My papa was right; I was with another man. I told Papa we were married and he exploded. Anton and I were going to get married after things settled down, but we didn't get the chance. Anton supposedly died in an accident, but I know Papa had him killed. We had a child together and we managed to hide it from my father. After Anton died, I brought him to the Mission and Martha has been raising him for me."

"You have a child? Does he know about you?" interrupted Joshua.

Angelina let a tear slip down her cheek. "Yes, he knows he has a mother living in the city, but no . . . he doesn't know yet that it is me."

"This must rip your heart out each time you come here, Angelina. I'm so sorry." Joshua wanted to gather her into his arms and hold her.

CHAPTER TWENTY-THREE

"Please, I must finish. This is so hard to tell a complete stranger, but somehow it's like I've known you all my life. I have worked for my father delivering packages for people all over Mexico. It's very dangerous work and several times I wanted out. Papa's tactics are very brutal so for relief from that lifestyle, I would hide here at the Mission. Martha is like the mother I never knew. She introduced me to her Savior. I can't go back into my old life, Joshua. After I met and spent time with Doug and Cynthia, we came up with the plan. I have kept it from Martha, not wanting any danger to come to the Mission or her. My father is very wicked and if he knew anything, he could make life very unpleasant for everyone here."

"Do you still love Anton, Angelina?"

Angelina paused before answering, "I thought he still had a place in my heart until I met you. Do you believe there is love at first sight?"

Joshua reached for her hand and noticed she, too, was still wearing her ring. "I'm beginning to think so. I was very much in love with my fiancée who died in an accident several months ago. But I've let her go and now I believe a new love has taken her place."

WHEN TWO WORLDS COLLIDE

Joshua pulled Angelina to her feet and bent his face down towards hers. He gently placed his lips on hers. He thought his heart would burst with love for her after the kiss ended. Her face was glowing and her eyes glistened with tears.

"I will be a good wife to you, Joshua."

"And I will be a good husband to you, Angelina. I want you to tell your son who you are, so we can take him to the United States to live with us."

"Joshua, are you sure? Can you love another man's child?"

Joshua was thinking about his mom and dad. They loved him like their own even though he wasn't. "Yes, I can, Angelina. I've been loved and cared for by two people and I'm not biologically their son either. I'll have to tell you my story too, Angelina. Now, let's go find your son."

Angelina put her arms around Joshua and hugged him tightly. God was the giver of good things!

CHAPTER TWENTY-FOUR

Martha met Angelina and Joshua coming out of her office. "I see you have sorted out your differences."

"Yes, Martha," said Joshua. "Thanks for the advice."

"Doug and Cynthia tell me you are leaving today. I will miss you, Angelina."

"Martha, I have some wonderful news. Joshua wants me to take my son to live with us in America."

"Oh Angelina, that's wonderful! Manuel was just asking the other day when he can see his mother."

"Manuel is your child?" asked Joshua surprised by this revelation.

Angelina looked at Joshua. "Yes, he is."

Angelina then turned to Martha. "Can I go get him at school and talk to him about coming with us?"

"What about your father, Angelina?

WHEN TWO WORLDS COLLIDE

He'll have his men watching the Mission by now."

In all the excitement, Angelina forgot for a time the grave danger she was actually in. Her heart sank within her. "You're right Martha, we must be careful not to endanger Manuel's life. I'll wait until he comes home this afternoon."

"But by the sounds of things, you will already be in America."

"I can't leave without my son, Martha."

Angelina looked to Joshua for support. "That's right, Martha," said Joshua, "we won't leave here without Manuel."

Just then Doug joined them. "Did I just hear you say you're not leaving here without your son, Angelina? I didn't know you had a son."

"No one but Martha knew. To keep him safe, I could tell no one."

Doug sighed. "This gets more complicated day by day. We have an appointment with detective Jose in San Diego at three this afternoon. I think then, that Cynthia and I should keep the appointment. It's probably too dangerous right now for Joshua and Angelina to leave the Mission. We'll find out what plans Jose has, and then let you know tomorrow. Joshua,

CHAPTER TWENTY-FOUR

I'll pick up the forms for your annulment. Cynthia and I have some shopping to do so we will stay one night in San Diego." Doug glanced at his watch, "We better be going. See you later."

Angelina and Joshua looked at each other and smiled. "Doug, don't worry about getting those papers, Angelina and I are staying married."

"What are you talking about?" Doug saw Martha frown and decided he better explain what he meant. "Martha, now don't get angry, but Cynthia and I thought this would be the best way to get Angelina to safety. The marriage wasn't suppose to last, they were to get an annulment in San Diego as soon as we left Mexico."

"Doug, I can't believe you would be this way about such a sacred vow!" exclaimed Martha. "This is something you don't play around with. Did Joshua know of this arrangement before he arrived in Mexico?"

"No, just Angelina knew," said Doug sheepishly.

Martha stepped toward Angelina. "You knew and didn't tell me?"

"It was for your own safety, Martha. The less everyone knew, the better. But Joshua and I love each other, so it worked out well."

Relaxing somewhat, Martha said, "I teach the children to always speak the truth. God says in His Word, the truth will set us free. And now I find out my dearest friends don't tell me the truth. How can this be?"

Angelina reached out and put her arm around Martha's waist. "Please forgive me, Martha. I thought keeping this from you was for your own safety."

"Yes, please forgive us too," added Doug. "We should have let you in on the plan. Although with your convictions about marriage, our plan would not have succeeded. And Joshua, what are your mom and dad going to say when they find out you're married?"

"This didn't seem to bother you before, Doug. Why is it so different now?"

"Because you wouldn't have been married once we reached Canada; remember the annulment?"

Joshua took enjoyment from watching Doug squirm. Letting him off the hook, Joshua replied, "I know Mom and Dad will be pleased once they meet Angelina and her son."

Angelina's eyes misted when Joshua said the words.

CHAPTER TWENTY-FOUR

Martha looked puzzled once again. "I thought Doug and Cynthia were your parents, Joshua."

"They are, but I didn't grow up with them. Another couple raised me. Doug, you better be going, I'll tell Martha and Angelina the story."

Doug hurried away, looking for Cynthia.

After Joshua told his story to Martha and Angelina, he went back to his room to move his belongings. He would be sharing a room with Angelina, his wife, tonight. Joshua grabbed the book he was reading and went back to Martha's office. Martha was busy looking through some papers when he came in.

"Excuse me, Martha, but do you know the author of this book?"

"Yes. She came with a group of young people from Cochrane to help build a house for a family here in Tijuana. Do you like the book?"

"Yes, I'm enjoying it."

"I'm sure you can get a copy when you go to Cochrane. The copy you're holding is mine."

Joshua smiled. "I wasn't going to take it Martha. Can I read it while I'm here?"

It was Martha's turn to smile. "Do you

WHEN TWO WORLDS COLLIDE

think you will have time to read it, Joshua?"

Joshua felt heat rise in his face. "May be I'll just leave it here with you, then."

Joshua and Martha laughed together. Joshua put his hands in his pockets and looked down at the floor. "May be I'll go see what Angelina is doing. Do you know where she is?" he asked looking up.

Martha nodded. "We've fixed up a room for you near the chapel. She's probably there."

Joshua left the office and walked through the courtyard to where the chapel was located. He found a flight of stairs and walked up them. At the top of the landing he noticed a door ajar and looked in. Angelina was putting her belongings in a dresser drawer. Joshua snuck in and put his arms around her. Angelina jumped and then trembled in Joshua's arms.

"Angelina . . . Angel" whispered Joshua softly, "you truly are my Angel. Want to take a nap?"

Angelina giggled. "It's morning, Joshua."

"We're married, we can take a nap anytime we want to." Joshua went over and shut the door.

CHAPTER TWENTY-FIVE

Luis Cortez had called a meeting of all his guards. His voice boomed throughout the room. "Are you trying to tell me that no one saw them trying to escape? And you Pedro, you were stationed right at their door. Where were you? I pay the highest wages in this city and I get these kinds of results? I want you to look for them, and don't come back here without them!"

One of the guards dared to ask a question. "You want us all to go? Who will guard you then?"

"You imbecile, I can look after myself, now get out of here!"

Everyone quickly left and Luis Cortez paced.

"You will not get away Angelina, so why do you try? Tijuana is a large city, but my contacts will find you and bring you back to me." Luis spoke out loud to an empty room. The phone rang and with no one else to answer it, he picked it up.

"Yes, I'll be in shortly, commander."

Luis placed the phone down and gritted his teeth until the side of his face twitched. There was no meeting scheduled today. Why did the commander want to see him? Were his business deals beginning to unravel right before his eyes? It was Angelina's fault; she would pay for this! What other person could look after her like he did. She didn't want for anything. Luis glanced down at his watch and realized he had better not keep his boss waiting.

Doug and Cynthia sat across the desk from Jose Armando. "Do you think, with my contacts in Tijuana, Angelina and Joshua will go back to the Cortez place? I believe this is the only way we can bust up the drug ring. Cortez by now will have his men looking for them. It might be to our advantage if they go back willingly. There must be one soft spot in this man."

Doug spoke next, "So you don't think it is dangerous? He could have them killed."

"I don't think he would do that, Doug. I think Mr. Cortez, even if he is twisted, loves his daughter. According to my sources,

CHAPTER TWENTY-FIVE

she's pulled off some pretty bizarre stunts, and Mr. Cortez has let her get away with them. After going through all my plans, Joshua and Angelina are the only ones who can walk into the Cortez place and plant the evidence. I still find it hard to believe that the commander has no idea about Luis Cortez's dealings throughout the years. But if this all works out, he will know soon enough. We don't want to move in too quickly, but with Joshua and Angelina on the premises, we can bide our time."

"What if Mr. Cortez's demands Joshua do something illegal?" asked Cynthia.

"We will deal with that if it becomes an issue."

"But," reminded Cynthia, "the laws in Mexico are different than here in the States, aren't they?"

Jose paused, thinking about Cynthia's question. "Yes, but my contacts will take the heat if something happens. I know your concerns are valid, Cynthia, so I'm coming back to the Mission with you both. I'm looking forward to seeing Martha again."

"How do you know Martha?" asked Doug.

"I lived there until I reached seventeen. A family from Canada sponsored me so I

WHEN TWO WORLDS COLLIDE

was able to go to college in the States. Martha was the mother I never had. The Mission was my only family," replied Jose fondly.

Cynthia smiled, "Martha has many children."

Angelina and Joshua sat a few tables away from Manuel as Martha spoke to him, while he ate an after school snack. With a bite in his mouth, he turned around quickly, and tears sprang into his eyes. He ran into Angelina's open arms.

"You're really my mama?" cried Manuel, hugging her tightly. "I prayed you would come for me."

Angelina could hardly breathe for the joy filling her. Her family was now complete.

Joshua closed his eyes and began to pray. *"What joy must come to Your heart Father, to see a family reunited. Please help me be a good father to Manuel and a good husband to Angelina. Your words are true in Jeremiah,* **'For I know the thoughts that I think toward you, says the Lord, thoughts of peace and not of evil, to give you a future and a hope.'**[11] *Help me to keep my eyes fixed upon You. I trust You to keep me in all my ways."*

[11] Jeremiah 29:11

CHAPTER TWENTY-FIVE

Joshua opened his eyes then to find Angelina and Manuel looking at him.

"Joshua, I'd like you to meet my son . . . our son, Manuel," introduced Angelina.

Manuel stuck out his little hand but Joshua scooped him up into his arms. "I'm so happy to know you, Manuel. We are going to have a wonderful life together."

Manuel questioned Angelina with his eyes. She spoke in Spanish to answer him.

Joshua then said, "I'll teach you how to speak English, if you teach me how to speak Spanish. Deal?"

Angelina spoke to him again and Manuel nodded.

Just then a police car pulled into the courtyard. Angelina's heart began to race, fear trying to capture her. When Cynthia and Doug emerged from the vehicle, Angelina breathed a sigh of relief.

Joshua noticed her fear and put his arm around her shoulder. "Don't worry, Angelina, I'll protect you."

Angelina looked over at him and smiled. Joshua didn't know what her father was capable of so she kept still. As she watched Doug, Cynthia, and the policeman approach, she still looked on with apprehension.

WHEN TWO WORLDS COLLIDE

After a homecoming celebration for Jose, the adults retired to Martha's office to discuss the business at hand.

Jose began, explaining the plan to Joshua and Angelina.

"You're saying, then, Angelina and I just walk back into the hellhole we were delivered from?"

Jose nodded. "You are the only two who have access to his residence." Jose locked eyes with Angelina, "We have spent almost a year trying to find a way to break this drug ring. Now it is so close, I can taste it. No charges will be laid against you, Angelina, if you co-operate with us."

Angelina then realized that even if her past was securely under the blood of Christ, she would still have to reap what she sowed. She thought about her new life and hoped she would one day be able to live it. Yes, she would help even if it meant her papa would have to spend time in prison for his evil deeds.

"Look, Detective Jose, I won't allow Angelina to be in any danger. Why can't I just go back in there?"

"Because it'll take both of you to convince Mr. Cortez you'll be willing to work for him. With you on his side, Joshua, he'll see

CHAPTER TWENTY-FIVE

a liaison between both countries. We're counting on him thinking this way. This may take time, but it will be worth the wait. Do you think you can convince him?"

Joshua didn't like the scenario one bit. It sounded dangerous and he was probably in over his head. What if something went wrong? He didn't want to see his life with Angelina suddenly cut short. Suddenly he heard the Lord whisper to his inner ear, ***"Joshua, I will be with you. You can do all things through Me, for I Am your strength. As you wait upon Me, I will instruct you and lead you in the paths you are to walk. I will make a way. Be still and know that I Am God."***

Joshua stood up. "Angelina and I will let you know in the morning. We'd like to spend some time with our son now, so excuse us."

Jose stood on his feet too and watched them leave the office. "I'm not too good at praying, but now would seem a good time to start. Martha, could you lead us please?"

Martha spoke to her Heavenly Father on behalf of the people involved in the scheme to oust evil from her city. She spoke in Spanish and Cynthia was able to understand some, but not all of her words. She prayed with much authority and all present knew she had the ear of God. When she was finished she looked at Jose. "This is a good time for you to rededicate yourself to the Lord. We are living in evil times and you need to be in God's army."

"I know, Martha, I know. In my line of work, I see so much darkness, evil seems to permeate the very air I breathe. I do need God's touch once again."

Martha stepped over to him and laid her hand on his shoulder. She spoke again in Spanish and when Jose lifted his head, a new light seemed to glow from his eyes. Jose felt like a heavy burden was lifted from his soul. "Gracias, Martha, gracias."

"No, it's not me, Jose, you should be thanking," instructed Martha. "God is the only one who can set the captive free."

After tucking Manuel into his bed, Angelina and Joshua went to their room and sat on the edge of their bed.

"We must be in total agreement if we're going to deceive your father, Angelina."

"I know Joshua. My father is very clever, so we must be very convincing."

"Angelina, we need to pray. The Lord is

CHAPTER TWENTY-FIVE

the only one who can deliver us from this evil." Joshua began to pray quietly in the Holy Spirit's language. He felt a boldness come suddenly into his spirit and began to speak loudly to the evil. He stood up and began to pace the room, taking authority over evil spirits. After doing this warfare, Joshua began to sing softly, the Holy Spirit giving him the words to sing.

Angelina began to weep quietly at first, and then loud sobs erupted. "I forgive my papa for all the things he has done to me. Please forgive me Jesus, for the part I played in all his evil work. I surrender my heart totally to You, Father God."

Joshua reached for his wife and they clung to each other. After sometime Angelina drew back from Joshua. "Please," she pleaded, "I would like to speak in this heavenly language too."

"You haven't been baptized in the Holy Spirit since you've believed?"

Angelina shook her head. "No, but I desire this."

"Just lift your hands and ask the Holy Spirit to come, Angelina, it's that simple."

Angelina lifted her hands and cried, "Holy Spirit, please come and fill me. I ask for this new language. Please, I need You!"

WHEN TWO WORLDS COLLIDE

Before Angelina spoke her last word, her heart began to burn. Her tongue began to tremble and as she opened her mouth, words she didn't understand came forth. It felt like a bubbling at first, then a flow of words swept her away. She felt like she could fly, soaring up on eagles' wings, as the scripture said. Her heart felt like it would burst with the love she experienced.

Joshua looked on with thankfulness. The oneness he experienced with Angelina was what the scriptures declared: ***"Have you not read that He who made them at the beginning made them male and female, and said, 'For this reason a man shall leave his father and mother and be joined to his wife, and the two shall become one flesh? So then, they are no longer two but one flesh. Therefore what God has joined together, let not man separate.*** [12]*"*

[12] Matthew 19:4-6

CHAPTER TWENTY-SIX

The cab driver spoke rapidly to Angelina and Joshua before he left them in front of the Cortez residence.

"What did he say?" asked Joshua.

"He wanted to know if we were both loco. He wondered if we knew Mr. Cortez and how dangerous the man was," replied Angelina. "I told him we were family."

"Well here goes, Angelina, and remember . . . if God is for us, who can be against us? We are in God's secret place and the wicked one touches us not."

Angelina gripped Joshua's hand firmly and nodded. As they approached the front door it suddenly flew open and Luis Cortez stood with a startled look on his face.

"Who found you? Who brought you here?" asked Luis his eyes searching his property.

"No one, Papa. We came here ourselves," replied Angelina.

Luis Cortez looked reluctant to believe her, but the fact of the matter was they were both standing in his doorway.

"So you came to your senses, did you? You knew I would find you sooner or later. Now get in here; we have work to do!"

Mr. Cortez ushered them into his office. "I don't know what happened to Hermosa, but she left here just after you did. Why do you think she would do this, Angelina?"

"She had a better job offer?"

"Don't be smart. She's been with this family since your mother died and I've paid her well. So, you're telling me you don't know where she is?"

"No, I don't know where she is, Papa. I'll miss her."

Mr. Cortez flipped through some papers on his desk and glared at Angelina.

"You better be telling me the truth, daughter. You know how I hate liars."

"So, Joshua, how do you like married life so far?"

"I love your daughter, Mr. Cortez. She was handpicked by God Himself."

Mr. Cortez threw back his head and laughed loudly, "Now that's funny! I don't

CHAPTER TWENTY-SIX

believe in God. And for him to handpick my daughter for you, now that's really something. Enough chatter, tonight you both will make a run. Angelina can show you the ropes, Joshua. Be back here in one hour or I'll be out there to deal with you myself!"

Angelina and Joshua left the office and headed towards their room. "I don't like this," began Joshua, when Angelina put her finger to her lips and motioned for him not to speak. After they were in their room and in the bathroom, Angelina whispered, "Joshua, you must be careful not to speak unless we are in here. Papa has his entire residence bugged. The only places he has not bugged are the bathrooms. I've checked it out. Now, we must get ready; Papa is not a patient man."

"Get ready? I thought I'd wear what I have on."

Angelina smiled. "That would be fine if we were going riding, Joshua, but we are dealing with influential business men."

"So, what do I wear then?"

Angelina took Joshua to the closet. "I see Papa has been busy. He must have known your size and purchased these clothes."

"I guess he could have taken my measurements. I was blacked out most of the

WHEN TWO WORLDS COLLIDE

time. And the clothes I found before Hank rescued us, he must have bought those ones too."

She pulled out a suit and matched it with a shirt and tie. Finding some shiny black shoes, she put them beside the bed. She then went to her own closet and brought out her clothes.

When Joshua had finished dressing, he waited for Angelina to come out of the bathroom. Angelina came out wearing clothes that made Joshua gasp.

"You can't wear those clothes in public, Angelina. I won't have men ogling you. Can't we find you something more appropriate?"

"I'm not a streetwalker, if that is what you think, Joshua. But this is what I have to wear when I'm out on a run. Please remember, I also have on God's full armor and the wicked one does not touch me."

"I'm sorry, Angelina," whispered Joshua in her ear. "I didn't mean to imply you were, you know . . . a streetwalker, but I don't want anyone else to touch you, either."

"We must trust God to look after us, Joshua. Now let's go."

Joshua thought for a moment and then took Angelina's hand. *"Father, we place our-*

CHAPTER TWENTY-SIX

selves into Your hands. Thank You for Your protection. We know You will lead and guide us. We are imprinted on the palms of Your hands."

Luis Cortez listened to the prayer and sneered. What kind of a religious nut had his daughter gotten tangled up with? Yet Angelina looked better than before. Maybe married life agreed more with her than he gave it credit. This was going to be good, very good, to have them doing business for him in America. His boss was asking too many questions lately and after this run he would do more of his business in the States. He wondered why his men hadn't been able to find Angelina and Joshua. How could they have just disappeared and then resurface willingly? He would have to interrogate Angelina later.

Angelina placed the parcel on her father's desk and watched him open it. Three large plastic bags were revealed. Luis opened one and put a small amount of the white powder on his fingertip. He put the powder into his mouth and smiled.

"Very good. Good job, both of you. In three days I will have a driver take you to San Diego. I've set up a delivery meeting for you. By the way, I've had the cameras removed from your room. I know you need privacy and if you continue to co-operate I'll give you more freedom."

Joshua and Angelina looked at each and couldn't believe what they were hearing. Why this sudden change in Luis? Angelina would make sure she checked their room thoroughly before she would believe her father. What was he up to?

"You have the next three days off. Angelina, I'll have a driver available to you. Why don't you take Joshua to the ranch? I'd like him to see some of my horses. Then you can show him around Tijuana. I'm retiring, I'll see you both tomorrow."

Angelina and Joshua watched him leave and just looked at each other.

"What do you think this is all about, Angelina? I didn't know your father had a ranch."

"I'm just as surprised as you are, Joshua. He has never given me this kind of treatment before. His leash on me has been so short I've felt strangled at times. But we must stay alert; this could all be mind

CHAPTER TWENTY-SIX

games. He could turn on us suddenly. I don't trust him no matter what he gives us. And yes he has a ranch, though I've only been there a couple of times. He knows how much I love the place, so he has made sure I don't get to enjoy it. I love the freedom of riding a horse."

Joshua reached out and took Angelina in his arms. "We have a beautiful ranch in Montana, Angelina. Once we're finished here, you can ride all day if you like."

Luis Cortez listened intently to their conversation. A ranch in Montana . . . very interesting. He would have to find some contacts there. Mind games, Angelina, really, you are too dramatic. I know a good thing when I see it; this was a good business transaction. Moving his business into the States would be very profitable, very profitable indeed. Luis stifled a yawn and went toward his room.

Remembering they were still in the office, Angelina then knew her father had probably listened to their whole conversation. But it didn't matter, being in Joshua's arms and knowing God was looking after them began to erase the fear she felt toward her earthly father.

CHAPTER TWENTY-SEVEN

"I know I told you to have some time off Angelina, but something has come up and you have to deliver this package today," insisted Luis. "I will send you both to a resort when this deal is completed. I know you think I'm just toying with you, but I'm not. Can't a person have a change of heart?"

"Only if Jesus Christ is the reason for the heart change, Mr. Cortez. *Porque de tal manera amó Dios al mundo, que ha dado a su Hijo unigénito, para que todo aquel que en él cree, no se pierda, mas tenga vida eternal,*[13]" quoted Joshua.

"Be quiet, Joshua! I didn't know you could speak Spanish. I told you I didn't believe in God, so don't try and push your beliefs down my throat. Now Angelina, you will take the package to this address and wait until they give you a package in return. Do you understand?"

[13] John 3:16 (San Juan 3:16)

WHEN TWO WORLDS COLLIDE

Angelina nodded. Papa was back to his old self. Somehow she felt she could deal with him better this way.

"And, I want you to wear a business suit . . . not the clothes you wore the other night. We are dealing with a different league of people in San Diego and we must play the part."

First, Joshua was relieved. He hated those other clothes. But why the sudden change in plans? What was going down and would they have a chance to contact Jose? Feeling uneasy in his spirit, he hoped he would be able to spend some time in prayer before they left.

"Now, go get ready. You leave here in one hour. Oh by the way, do you know a Martha? She called here looking for you, Angelina."

Angelina tried not to look surprised. "Yes, she is a friend of mine. What did you tell her?"

"I told her you were out. She didn't want to leave a message so I told her to call back today. Who is this friend?"

"No one you know, Papa. You know how I love children. I helped her look after some children in a mission."

Luis stared intently at Angelina. "I'd like

CHAPTER TWENTY-SEVEN

to give some money to this mission. Where is it?"

"Look, if we have to leave here in an hour, we better get changed."

"Okay Angelina, so you don't want to tell me about the Mission, why is that? I want to help, so when you return we will go there together, understand?"

Angelina tried to smile. "Yes, Papa, we will go together."

Once they were back in their room, Angelina let the tears she was holding back slip down her cheeks. "Joshua, I didn't know you knew that much Spanish. What you spoke was John 3:16 wasn't it?"

Joshua nodded. "The Lord told me to open my mouth and He would fill it."

"I'm so afraid, though. Why would Martha call here? She knows how dangerous it is?"

"I don't think Martha would call, Angelina. What I think happened is that your father intercepted our note to Martha. I just pray Hermosa is really safe somewhere."

"Do you see how he plays mind games, Joshua? He has been speaking lies and I have believed them. Why didn't I see it?"

"Angelina, don't be so hard on yourself. I know you want to believe the best about

WHEN TWO WORLDS COLLIDE

your father, but until he truly has a heart change, he doesn't know how to speak the truth. Come on, let's get ready. We don't want to keep him waiting."

Angelina and Joshua prayed silently in the Spirit while they waited in line at the border. Angelina's fear totally subsided as she surrendered to the Holy Spirit. A border policeman took their passports and stared at them both. He then waved the driver on and Joshua breathed a sigh of relief. The driver spoke to Angelina in Spanish.

Angelina spoke. "He said that was the easiest border crossing he has ever experienced. Joshua, I feel something powerful will happen today."

"I know. I sense the same thing, Angelina. This whole ordeal could be over today. Do you sense the Presence of the Lord in this car?"

Angelina took Joshua's hand. "I do, Joshua, I really do!"

Their car sped along, but as they approached the address, a police car with lights flashing pulled them over. Their driver looked back at them, his face turning pale.

A policeman tapped on the window and the driver opened his window. "Drivers license and registration please."

CHAPTER TWENTY-SEVEN

"No speak English," replied the driver.

Angelina quickly spoke Spanish to the driver and he nodded. He fumbled around in the glove compartment and produced the items for the police officer.

Joshua opened his window and waited for the police officer to speak. "Everything seems to be in order. Where are you going?"

Angelina was wondering if the driver was bluffing about whether he could speak English or not. She just couldn't trust anyone who worked for her father. So she waited to see if the driver would answer. He turned around looking for help from Angelina.

"We have some business in San Diego and then we will be returning to Tijuana."

"Could I see your passports?"

Joshua handed them out the window and the officer went to his car. He returned shortly. "Tell the driver to wait here. Please follow me to my car?"

Angelina spoke to the driver. He gripped the steering wheel until his knuckles turned white. The driver slightly nodded as Angelina left the vehicle.

On the way to the car, Joshua asked, "Is there a problem, Officer?"

The officer didn't reply until they were

all seated in his car. "I have a message from Detective Jose. After delivering the package you will come with me to the station. I'm just waiting for back-up. We will take your driver into custody. You will not be in danger if you do exactly as you are instructed."

"And how do we know you are working for Jose?"

The officer thought for a moment and then handed Joshua his phone. "Call him."

"Can I please speak to Detective Jose Armando? Yes, I will hold. Jose? Joshua here. What's happening?"

"We've had a miracle, Joshua. Everything is going down today. While we speak, Mr. Cortez is being arrested for his dealings. We finally were able to convince the Commander about Mr. Cortez. It's good you are in San Diego and not in Tijuana right now. Just follow my officer's instructions and I will see you soon."

"Okay, and thanks Jose. This is quite a relief."

Joshua handed the phone back to the officer. "We're ready."

Just then another police car arrived on the scene. An officer walked over to the Mexican car and ordered the driver to step

CHAPTER TWENTY-SEVEN

out of the vehicle. The driver didn't budge. They watched as the officer forcefully pulled him from the vehicle and cuffed him. Another man dressed like the Mexican man took his place behind the wheel.

"Okay you two, showtime!"

Angelina and Joshua got out of the car and walked towards their vehicle. Angelina handed the driver the address and he started the car. At the building, Angelina and Joshua took their package in. Two men in business suits greeted them warmly and took them into an office. After inspecting the package, they handed Joshua a briefcase. No words were exchanged; Joshua just nodded. Suddenly the door flew open and uniformed police filled the office. The startled men didn't fight but gave up the package willingly. They were cuffed and taken to one of the cars. Angelina and Joshua were escorted to another car and soon they were on their way to see Jose.

"It seemed too easy," commented Joshua. "I think I expected a gunfight or something."

Jose smiled. "I think you watch too much television, Joshua."

"I don't watch any television, but I do

listen to the news. Guns and drug busts seem to go together."

"Yes, this is true, but we can thank God we didn't have to experience it. I've been seeing many changes because of prayer."

"I'm glad, Jose. Can Angelina and I go back into Tijuana? We have to get our son."

"It's too dangerous for you there right now. Until all of Cortez's men are rounded up, you'll have to stay in San Diego. Cynthia and Doug will bring Manuel to you."

Angelina finally spoke after realizing everything was really over. "What will happen to my father?"

Jose paused before speaking, "He will be in prison for a very long time, if he survives the gun shot wound. Things went down smoothly here, but not so in Tijuana."

"He's been shot? I must see him. He can't go off into eternity without Christ!"

"I'm sorry, Angelina, but it's too dangerous right now. Let's agree that God will send someone to speak salvation to him. I have you both booked into a hotel on Coronado Island. This is my way of saying thanks for helping us. You haven't had a very nice honeymoon so far, have you?"

"No," smiled Joshua. "But until our whole family is together, we can hardly enjoy ourselves."

CHAPTER TWENTY-SEVEN

"Don't worry about Manuel; he will be joining you shortly. You have my word on it."

Joshua reached for Jose's extended hand. "Thanks, we do appreciate your gift to us."

"What a gorgeous hotel," exclaimed Angelina with delight. "Look we have a wonderful ocean view!"

Joshua joined Angelina at the window and opened the door to their balcony. A salty wind blew on their faces and Joshua leaned down and kissed her. He lifted his head and announced, "Angelina, I need to call Mom and Dad. I want to introduce them to my new wife."

CHAPTER TWENTY-EIGHT

After several phone calls to Montana, Joshua finally heard a voice on the other end.

"Hello."

"Mom, hello, it's Joshua!"

"Oh Joshua, how are you?" exclaimed Belinda, surprised to hear his voice. She called to Dan to pick up the other phone.

"Joshua, it's good to hear your voice, son," added Dan.

"Good, you're both on the line. I have some wonderful news for you. I've recently gotten married."

There was a long pause and Belinda spoke first. "Joshua, before you say anything, can I tell you about the vision God gave me some time ago?"

"I'm listening, Mom."

"After Madison was taken home, the Lord showed me you would be married.

WHEN TWO WORLDS COLLIDE

The woman you married is dark-skinned and you already have a son who is about eight. In this vision your wife is holding a little girl and you are holding a little boy."

Joshua felt tears run down his cheeks. Angelina, seeing this, came and stood beside Joshua, putting her arms around his waist.

"Mom, Dad, her name is Angelina and we have a son whose name is Manuel. He is eight years old."

"Praise God, Joshua! He is the giver of good gifts. When can we meet them?"

"I'm bringing them to Montana first before we go to Canada. I think we can have things wrapped up here in about two weeks. So much has taken place. We are waiting for Manuel's passport and some other loose ends to be tied up. Mom, Dad, Angelina would like to speak with you."

Joshua then handed the phone to Angelina.

"Hello, Mr. and Mrs. Cole. I'm so happy to meet you. You have a wonderful son."

"Welcome to our family, Angelina," said Dan. "We are looking forward to the time we can spend together."

"Yes," added Belinda, "I'm very happy. Dan and I are looking forward to meeting you and your son."

CHAPTER TWENTY-EIGHT

Angelina handed the phone back to Joshua.

"Mom, Dad, I'll give you a call and let you know when you can expect us."

"Okay Joshua, and we miss you!"

"I miss you, too. See you in a couple of weeks, then. Oh yeah, right now we are staying in the Coronado Hotel. It's pretty nice."

"Isn't it expensive, Joshua?" questioned Belinda.

"It is Mom, but it's a gift from a new friend of ours."

"I'd like to meet your new friend," laughed Belinda.

"May be you will one day, Mom. I'd like you and Dad to visit the Mission, it's a miracle in progress."

"Joshua, Angelina sounds so sweet. We can hardly wait to see you both . . . and your new son."

"I'm looking forward to showing them off too, Mom. Dad, see you soon!"

There was a unison of goodbyes as Joshua hung up the phone.

Joshua reached for Angelina and held her close. "Do you want to hear something unbelievable, only it truly happened?"

Angelina smiled up at him. "Si!"

"The Lord gave my mom a vision of my

new family. She described you and said we had a son who was eight years old."

"Really, Joshua. That's amazing!"

"And that's not all. She said you were holding a little girl and I was holding a little boy. Do you think God is going to give us twins?"

"It would have to be a miracle, Joshua. I don't know of anyone in our family who has had twins!"

Joshua laughed. "Nor I in mine. I'll have to ask Doug and Cynthia though, if there have been twins in their family. I don't know the history of their family tree yet."

"I'm beginning to think God has much in store for us, Joshua. I've been thinking about Papa. I wonder if he is still alive?"

"I'll give Jose a call. May be he can enlighten us."

Joshua dialed the number and after several minutes of waiting to be transferred, Jose was on the line.

"Hello Joshua. I've been meaning to call but have been tied up with another case I've been working on. Mr. Cortez has been asking to see Angelina. I've spoken to the Commander there and he says he will allow it. All charges have been dropped against Angelina so she is free to go back into

CHAPTER TWENTY-EIGHT

Tijuana. I must say though, this is a miracle. I guess I had no idea how involved she really was. But not to worry now, her slate has been wiped clean. I'll send a car for you. Can you be ready in an hour?"

"Yes Jose, we can. Do you know if Manuel's passport is ready?"

"It's still being processed but should be ready in a day or two. And you have your room at the hotel for another week."

"This is a wonderful place, Jose. Thank you so much for your generosity."

"You're welcome, Joshua. Manuel will be able to enjoy it too. There's lots of sightseeing to be done while you're in San Diego."

"Yes, we've been looking at the brochures in our room. We're thinking of driving him to Disneyland."

"I'm sure he'll have fun. My kids have a ball there. Well, I better run. I'll see you in an hour."

Joshua hung up and walked to the balcony where Angelina was enjoying the scenery.

"Jose is taking us to Tijuana. He'll be here in an hour."

Angelina turned towards him. "Is it Papa? Is he still alive?"

WHEN TWO WORLDS COLLIDE

"Yes, Angelina. He's been asking for you. Jose also said that all charges have been dropped against you. You are free to go back to Tijuana."

Tears glistened in Angelina's eyes. "Joshua, God is faithful. He is truly someone you can depend upon. I'm learning to put my full trust in Him. He has not let me down yet. His love does cover a multitude of sins."

"I believe God will use us in Tijuana. As we wait upon Him, He will lead and guide us. And yes, Angelina, God is faithful! He is not a man that He would lie. He is true to His Word."

Angelina was quiet on the way back to Tijuana. Joshua used the time to pray and seek direction from the Lord. His heart ached for the Mexican people. He wanted to be able to share Christ's freedoms with them. As he prayed, he asked the Lord to give him opportunities to share the gospel.

The car soon pulled up to a building and stopped. Jose led the way and they soon found themselves in a small room.

Angelina looked at the form lying on

CHAPTER TWENTY-EIGHT

the bed, but didn't recognize the man. His face was ashen and tubes protruded from his body. Every time he breathed, his face wrenched in pain. Angelina approached the bed and looked into his face. Tears slid down her cheeks as she watched his agony. She reached out and slipped her hand into his.

"Papa," whispered Angelina, "I'm here."

The man opened his eyes slowly at the sound of her voice. Until his eyes could focus, he kept silent. Thank you God, he breathed to himself. He then struggled to speak. "Angelina, please forgive me," he rasped.

"I have forgiven you, Papa. But please don't go off into eternity without Christ. Jesus wants to forgive you if you accept Him into your heart. I will pray this prayer and will you agree with me for your salvation?"

Luis Cortez took another painful breath and whispered, "Yes, pray for me."

On hearing this, Joshua came and stood with Angelina, holding her other hand. Jose bowed his head.

Angelina began, *"Jesus, I know I'm a sinner and I ask You to forgive me. I know You are the Son of God and You came to reconcile me back to Father God. You stand at the door of my heart knocking. Please come in and take control of my life. Thank You for dying on the cross so I can have eternal life."*

Luis gripped Angelina's hand. Tears slipped down his whiskered cheeks. He then looked at Joshua. "Look after my little girl."

"I will, Mr. Cortez. As you know, God chose her for me and we will look after each other."

Luis could no longer speak. He locked his eyes on Angelina's face and wished he had made the decision before. His life would have been different. He would have been a good father. *"God, how I've wasted my life. Thank you for bringing Angelina here before I died. Thank you."* Luis gripped her hand once more before slipping away.

Angelina stroked his face. "Goodbye, Papa."

Angelina leaned on Joshua, placing her head on his chest and wept silently. Joshua held her close and looked down at Luis Cortez. Instead of agony there was peace. Joshua knew, only God could give man this kind of peace.

After leaving the infirmary, Jose turned around to speak to Angelina. "The commander wants to have a word with you before you pick up Manuel."

CHAPTER TWENTY-EIGHT

"I thought I was free from all charges, Jose," said Angelina, fear trying to grip her heart.

"Don't be afraid, Angelina. He has some papers to give you after they went through your father's residence. Did you know that he is a Christian?"

"No, Jose, I didn't know. He attends a church, then?"

"He's not religious, if that's what you're implying. He is born again. We've had quite a few discussions since I've come to know him better. He's been praying for your father for many years."

"Why didn't he know about my father's affairs, if he was a Christian?"

"I asked him the same question myself. He said he shut down after one of his children had been killed, and just let someone else do the work. That someone, of course, was your father. He says he has asked for forgiveness and is now allowing the Lord to lead and guide him. Since this drug ring has been exposed, three men have been saved."

"That's good news!" said Joshua, encouraged by what Jose was sharing.

"Yes, it is. Here we are now," said Jose, looking out the window. "We'll come in with you, but I know the commander wants to speak with you alone, Angelina."

WHEN TWO WORLDS COLLIDE

Joshua began to say something, but Angelina put her hand on his arm, "It's okay, Joshua, God will be with me. I must speak to him alone."

Joshua stood with Jose as Angelina walked through the doors leading to the commander's office.

Commander Samuel Fernando extended his hand to Angelina as she approached his desk.

"Please sit down."

Angelina sat down and clasped her hands together.

"After going through your father's residence, we discovered these papers. It seems your father will be leaving you his estate. Because of his illegal dealings, we've had to search all the premises. We did find some items at his ranch, but we have confiscated them. I've just been informed that your father has died. Please accept my sympathies."

"Thank you. I don't know if I have a right to those properties. I'm sure they have been purchased with blood money. My Papa did many wicked things."

"I know Angelina. But I believe God can turn what was meant for evil into something good. I know of your conversion to Christ.

CHAPTER TWENTY-EIGHT

You can now use these properties for something good. It says somewhere in God's word, He gives us beauty for ashes. Would you like to retain my lawyer for probating the will?"

Angelina sat in awe listening to Commander Fernando speak God's Word. Their city was in good hands. "Yes, that would be fine, Commander Fernando."

"If there is anything I can do for you Angelina, please let me know. I would appreciate your prayers, as I need direction in administering justice. We still have much work to do in rooting out the evil in our city," he said standing up.

Angelina stood as well. "You can count on Joshua and I praying for you daily, Commander Fernando."

He smiled. "Thank you, Angelina."

Angelina left his office, thanking God for His provision.

After settling themselves into the car once again, Angelina began to talk about the meeting with Samuel Fernando.

"It seems my father willed me all his land holdings and the residence in Tijuana. I told him I didn't think I had a right to those properties because of my father's dealings. Commander Fernando said he believed

WHEN TWO WORLDS COLLIDE

God could bring beauty out of the ashes. After the will is probated, Commander Fernando's lawyer will release Papa's estate to me. I still find it hard to believe all charges were dropped against me."

"Did you willingly agree to do all the work your father gave you to do?" asked Jose.

"No, but after awhile I didn't question anything. I just did what my father instructed. He could be very convincing."

"I can't imagine the abuse you endured Angelina. Even though he's come to Christ, I'm glad he can no longer hurt you," sympathized Jose. "I'm going to drop you two off at the Mission. I need to get back to my office. I'll send my driver back for you later if that's okay."

"Yes, thank you for all your help," replied Joshua. "We'll get all of Manuel's things together and be ready when he returns."

Once at the Mission, Manuel sat with Angelina and Joshua, not wanting to let go of them. Angelina spoke softly to him in Spanish. "We're a family now, Manuel. You'll be living with us. Before we go to Joshua's place in Montana we are taking you to an exciting place called Disneyland. We will have so much fun together!"

CHAPTER TWENTY-EIGHT

"We went on a trip to San Diego once. Sister Martha took us to the Zoo. That was fun!"

"I know Martha has been so good to you. We will miss her but we will come back and visit with her, okay?"

Manuel nodded and snuggled up against Angelina once again.

Martha joined them later, and several people Joshua did not know accompanied her. "Joshua, I'd like you to meet the rest of my family. This is Seth, one of my sons and his wife Lilia; my other daughter Susana and her husband Ramon, and Rosalinda . . . who has been like a daughter to me."

Joshua greeted them all. "It's a pleasure to meet you. Do you all work here at the Mission?"

Seth spoke on behalf of his family. "We do. I work in administration at an office in San Diego and my sisters and wife work here with the children. Ramon works in construction and helps with many of the building projects. We're just one big happy family," laughed Seth. "What do you do in Montana, Joshua?"

"I'm a pastor. I also do some ranching, helping my dad."

WHEN TWO WORLDS COLLIDE

Angelina looked surprised. "You're a pastor, Joshua? No wonder you know so much about the Bible."

Joshua smiled. "We have many things to share with one another, Angelina. I don't look at this title as being as important as my walking in Christ is. I want people to see me as a child of God doing those things which please Him."

"That is a wise thing to say," said Martha, "but you also do not want to be ashamed. God has called you and anointed you for this position and people need to know it."

Joshua thought for a moment before answering, "Thank you Martha, for your insight. I will remember your words to me."

Soon Martha's family was speaking to one another in Spanish. Joshua and Angelina excused themselves and put Manuel's belongings in a bag. Because everyone shared in the clothing given to the Mission, Manuel didn't have many things. Joshua would remedy this as soon as they were back in San Diego.

Manuel wrapped his arms around Martha's neck and hugged her tightly.

Martha hugged him back. "You be a good boy for your mom and new Papa,

CHAPTER TWENTY-EIGHT

Manuel. God go with you and watch over you."

"Thank you for taking care of Manuel. We'll be back to visit you, Martha. Joshua and I want to put my father's land to good use."

Angelina and Joshua hugged her too.

Doug and Cynthia had returned to Canada. The plan was for Joshua and Angelina to join them after their trip to Montana. Joshua remembered the conversation he had with Doug. Just after exchanging vows with Angelina in Mexico, he told Doug they would be going to Montana first. Now he wondered if the words had been prophetic.

CHAPTER TWENTY-NINE

Belinda and Dan waited anxiously for Joshua's plane to arrive. After speaking to them once again from San Diego, they knew the flight number and approximate arrival time. Excitement welled up in Belinda as she watched the planes landing from her window viewpoint. She glanced over to Dan who was reading a magazine. Belinda walked over and sat beside him. "I'm so excited, I can't sit still. How can you keep so calm?"

Dan looked up from the magazine and smiled. "I'm excited too, Belinda, but guess I deal differently with it. I've been thinking about Edward and Joan. I pray they will be able to handle this news of Joshua's. It's only been a year since the accident."

"I know, Dan. I actually saw Joan in town the other day and we spoke briefly.

WHEN TWO WORLDS COLLIDE

She asked about Joshua and said she'd been praying for him. You can still see the ache in her eyes, Dan. When I thought I was losing Joshua, it felt like my heart would break. I can't imagine what she experiences daily."

Dan's heart swelled with love for Belinda. She had changed so much during this past year; he felt sometimes he was married to a different woman. God truly had set her free. He reached out and put his arm around her shoulder and pulled her closer to him. "Belinda, God will give Joshua the right words to speak. It may be hard at first for Joan and Edward, but I believe they will accept Angelina. Edward shared at the men's group that after the accident he didn't feel he would ever get over his heartache and loneliness for Madison. He did say he spends more time in God's word and he doesn't take things in his life for granted anymore. He said he has learned to seek first God's kingdom realities before the things of this earth. After he shared, many men there rededicated their lives to Christ. The Lord has given Edward and Joan a ministry for grieving couples."

Belinda looked over at the door where they expected Joshua and his new family

CHAPTER TWENTY-NINE

to come through. Looking at the arrival screen, she noticed the plane had landed.

"Dan, let's go wait by the door. His plane has arrived."

Dan laughed. "Okay, I've finished reading the magazine anyway!"

Belinda playfully punched Dan in the arm. "You didn't come here to read a magazine, Dan Cole!"

Belinda held the bouquet of flowers to give Angelina, her heart beating rapidly each time the doors opened. Soon she spotted Joshua and practically threw the flowers at Dan. She ran to meet Joshua, flinging her arms around his neck.

"Joshua, it's so good to see you. Welcome home!"

Joshua held on to her and then stepped back. Dan reached the two and noticed a petite woman and a small boy standing a few steps behind them. He stepped towards them and extended his hand. "Hello, Angelina, I'm Joshua's dad."

Angelina shook his hand and then looked down at Manuel. "And this is our son, Manuel."

The boy shyly looked at Dan. Dan knelt down so he was eye level with Manuel. "Hola Manuel!"

WHEN TWO WORLDS COLLIDE

Manuel beamed when he heard his language.

"Sorry, that's about all I know."

Joshua reached for his dad and hugged him. He put his arm around Angelina. "Mom, Dad, this is my new wife, Angelina and our son Manuel."

Belinda went over and hugged Angelina. She also knelt down and hugged Manuel. "It's so nice to meet you and we are thankful you are part of our family. Dan and I have been looking forward to the day when we would be grandparents." Belinda stroked Manuel's face and then hugged him again.

Angelina told Manuel what Belinda had said. Manuel quickly put his hand in Belinda's.

"While Dad and I wait for the bags, why don't you take Angelina and Manuel to the vehicle, Mom?"

"Good idea, Joshua." Belinda then remembered the flowers and, taking them from Dan, handed them to Angelina.

"Oh how beautiful, Mrs. Cole. Thank you so much!"

Belinda walked with them to where the van was parked, still holding Manuel's hand. She showed Angelina and Manuel where to sit.

CHAPTER TWENTY-NINE

Dan and Joshua soon joined them. "Hey, I didn't know you guys had a van," said Joshua, surprised by the new vehicle.

"We borrowed it from Peter and Stacey," said Dan. "I knew we wouldn't all fit in the truck."

Manuel then whispered something to Angelina and she smiled. "Manuel was telling me the Mission has a van but everyone must sit very close together to fit in."

Joshua struggled with a few words in Spanish to Manuel, who laughed. Joshua reached over and stroked him on the head. "Manuel has been teaching me some Spanish but I'm not very good with my pronunciation yet. He thinks I sound funny."

"I think you are doing very well, Joshua," encouraged Angelina. "You'll be speaking Spanish before we go back to Tijuana."

Joshua bent his head and brushed his lips on Angelina's cheek. Belinda watched Joshua's affection and his gentleness almost moved her to tears. What a miracle, Father, she thought to herself. Just a year ago his heart was shattered and now here he was with a family of his own.

After Joshua showed Angelina and Manuel around the house and the barns near the house, they tucked Manuel in. Manuel couldn't believe he could stay in a room this size by himself; he looked small in the large bed. By the time prayers were said, Manuel could hardly keep his eyes open.

Joshua and Angelina stood at his door until they knew he was sleeping. "This has been one long day," yawned Joshua. "Mom has some hot chocolate for us in the kitchen. Would you like some?"

Angelina smiled. "That is very thoughtful of her. Yes, Joshua, that would be nice."

In the kitchen Dan and Belinda sat next to each other waiting for Angelina and Joshua.

Joshua sipped his hot chocolate while Angelina shared her story with Dan and Belinda. Several times during her talk, Angelina would look at Joshua and reach for his hand. "I'm so very thankful God chose Joshua to be my husband. It is a miracle that my son and I have this man in our lives."

Belinda was blowing her nose, and Dan's eyes glistened with tears listening to the ordeal Angelina had been put through.

"Even though there is much tragedy with your story, Angelina," commented Belinda, "you are walking in victory. I'm sure the Lord has a wonderful ministry for

CHAPTER TWENTY-NINE

you both. You talked at the airport about going back to Tijuana; will you have a home there as well?"

"Joshua and I have discussed it and with the property my papa left me, we are considering starting a mission for children. Like I said, if it wasn't for Martha, I don't know what I would have done."

Belinda thought for a moment before she asked her next question. "Angelina, do you mind if I ask how old you are?"

"Mother, really!"

"That's okay Joshua. I'm twenty-four."

"You were quite young when you had Manuel, then," commented Belinda. "You were brave to take him and leave him at the Mission."

"Thank you Mrs. Cole, but I didn't feel very brave. I think I was motivated by fear more than anything else. If my papa had found out, I know he would have had me abort the baby. Anton and I were very much in love and were going to be married, but things drastically changed for both of us."

Joshua could see tiredness seep into Angelina. "Well, Angelina and I are going to bed, we're really quite tired."

"I'm sorry if we kept you up," apologized Dan.

WHEN TWO WORLDS COLLIDE

"It's okay Mr. Cole; I've enjoyed talking to you both. But I'm sorry I can't seem to keep my eyes open now."

Joshua stood up with Angelina and took her hand. "We've got lots of time to visit. Night Mom, night Dad."

"It's good to have you both home," Belinda said.

"So this is what Angelina and I are planning to do, Doug. Can you and your family come?"

Joshua could hear Doug explaining the idea to Cynthia. He came back to the phone momentarily. "I think we can all come Joshua and thanks for the invite. Your sisters are looking forward to meeting you."

Joshua thought for a moment. "Skye and Dakota, right?"

Doug laughed. "You remembered their names. Good Joshua."

Joshua didn't know how to take the comment so he just let it go.

"Angelina and I will pick you up on Saturday."

"Right, we'll see you then."

CHAPTER TWENTY-NINE

Joshua hung up the phone and sighed deeply.

"What's wrong Joshua . . . can't they come?" asked Belinda wiping her hands on a towel.

"Yes, they're coming, it's just that I don't know how to take some of Doug's comments. May be I'm trying too hard."

"Give it time, Joshua. They do seem like nice people."

Joshua smiled. "You sure have changed, Mom. I remember the times you wanted me all to yourself, always protecting your little boy."

Belinda smiled too. "My little boy can obviously look after himself. I have changed, Joshua, and thank you for noticing. The Lord has been really teaching me how to let go and rest in Him. My fretting over things just makes me unhappy. I want Him to be in control. He does a much better job than me."

"I had to learn that in Mexico. I would really like you and Dad to come down there when we're settled. You'll be thankful for even the air you breathe here."

"I'm so thankful God kept you safe even though you went through absolute hell. Our times of prayer and fasting for you were intense as well."

"Thanks Mom. I sure needed those prayers too."

Angelina heard Joshua speaking with his mother and decided to give them time together. She put on her shoes and coat and went to look for Manuel. After breakfast he had run outside to check out all the animals. Once outside Angelina took in the beauty of the Cole ranch. The house looked larger outside and Angelina especially liked the porch, which surrounded the entire house. A horse whinnied and Angelina went towards the sound. She reached out her hand and stroked his sleek neck.

"You are a beauty, aren't you?"

The horse seemed to want to show-off and began to prance around the corral. Angelina climbed the railed fence to watch him. He moved cautiously to her and let her pet him once again.

"Do you want to go for a ride?"

"Joshua, you scared me. I'd love to. Can I ride him?"

Joshua climbed up on the fence beside her. "Sure, but he looks like he's feeling his oats. Do you think you can handle him?"

Angelina smiled. "I'd like to try."

"All right then. Let's go saddle him up and I'll find a horse for myself. Is Manuel out here somewhere?"

CHAPTER TWENTY-NINE

"I hope so. I came looking for him, but the horse called out to me so I wanted to check him out first. May be he's with your dad."

"Let's check on him first and then we'll go for the ride."

Angelina nodded as Joshua lifted her down from the fence. "Your parents have a beautiful ranch! There are so many wide-open spaces. It's hard to believe only a few people live here."

After being in Tijuana those months Joshua knew what Angelina was saying. Yes, they were truly blessed to live where they were.

"We really don't know how blessed we are until we go into a place like Tijuana." Joshua thought for a moment before he continued. "I didn't mean to imply your city is bad, just overcrowded."

"In many ways it is evil, Joshua. It's just that there is such a contrast between places. Thank you for bringing me here."

Warmth covered Joshua and his heart burned. "Angel, I love you so much. God has blessed us with two homes so we can effectively help those in need."

"I love you too, Joshua. I'm so thankful we will be able to help some children in Tijuana. There is so much need."

WHEN TWO WORLDS COLLIDE

Just then Manuel came running towards them. "Mama, Mama," he shouted in Spanish. "Can I go with Grandpa to town? I get to ride in the big truck!"

Angelina and Joshua laughed. "Yes, Manuel. You be a good boy and do what you're told. Papa and I are going to ride the horses so we'll see you later."

Manuel suddenly looked sad.

"We'll take you for a ride tonight, Manuel," Joshua said quickly.

Angelina spoke to Manuel in Spanish. His eyes lit up again and he smiled. He then turned and ran towards the truck waiting for him.

Belinda watched Joshua and Angelina as they approached the house. She couldn't get over the miracle of them both. Belinda opened the door leading into the kitchen and waited for the two to step up to the veranda.

"I'd like to take Angelina dress shopping for next Sunday. Would that be all right?"

Joshua looked down at Angelina. "What do you think?"

CHAPTER TWENTY-NINE

"Oh yes, I would love to go shopping with you Mrs. Cole."

"Angelina, please call me Belinda . . . or Mom if you like. Mrs. Cole sounds too formal. You're family now."

Angelina's eyes quickly misted with tears. "I've never had a mother. Can I call you Mom?"

Belinda hugged her and whispered in her ear. "My daughter died at birth, so I would be delighted to have you call me Mom."

"I'm so sorry you lost your baby," sympathized Angelina.

"Thank you, Angelina. Now God has given me a new daughter."

"Okay you two, I'm going to see Pastor Ken. I'll see you in a couple of hours?"

"Yes," answered Belinda. "We should be finished by then."

Joshua kissed his wife goodbye and set off to visit with his friend. First though, he thought to stop and see Edward and Joan. He wanted to be the first to share the news of his marriage. Being that it was now later in the afternoon, he found them both at home.

"Joshua," greeted Joan, "it's so nice to have you home. How was your trip?"

"If you have a couple of hours, I can tell you all about it," smiled Joshua.

WHEN TWO WORLDS COLLIDE

Joan and Edward ushered Joshua into the living room and sat with him.

"Can I get you anything?" Joan asked.

"No thanks. It's good to see you both again. I have some news and I'm not sure how to tell you." Joshua asked the Lord for words and direction before he continued. "My time in Mexico turned out to be incredibly dangerous, but God's mercy and grace sustained me through it all. I walked through a fiery furnace but God delivered me." Joshua then shared his story and the horrid ordeal he endured.

Joan and Edward sat transfixed. In different parts of the story their faces looked at him in horror. When he was through, Joshua waited for their response.

Edward spoke first. "The Lord gave us such intense prayers for you Joshua, while you were away. But one thing we have been praying together is that God would send you a woman to love. It's too dangerous for us to hold on to the past. We must walk in today and look forward to what the Lord has planned for us. We would love to meet Angelina."

Joshua felt a great weight come off his heart. "Would you like to come to our marriage ceremony next Sunday? We want to renew our marriage vows with our family

CHAPTER TWENTY-NINE

and friends. We have papers of our marriage in Mexico, but we also want an American license as well."

"That's probably a good idea, Joshua." Edward looked at Joan who had kept silent as Edward talked. "Would you like to go, Joan?"

Tears collected in Joan's eyes and ran down her cheeks. "Madison loved you so much, Joshua. I know she would want to see you happy. We love you like a son, and yes, I would like to come to your wedding."

CHAPTER THIRTY

Angelina and Joshua now stood at the same door they had come through a week ago, waiting for Doug and Cynthia's plane to land. Soon Angelina was in Cynthia's arms as they cried together. Joshua gripped Doug's hand and looked around him to see two young women standing there.

"Joshua, this is Skye and Dakota."

Joshua went over and hugged them both. "Hi, guess we have some catching up to do," he laughed.

This seemed to put the girls at ease and they smiled back.

On the way home Angelina and Cynthia spoke to one another in Spanish while Doug and Joshua sat in the front. Skye and Dakota looked at one another, "This is going to be fun," said Dakota sarcastically.

WHEN TWO WORLDS COLLIDE

"I think it'll be fun," replied Skye, "I love weddings!"

"Yeah, right. Riding Flash around the barrels is fun, Skye . . . not watching two people getting hitched."

Joshua looked into the rear view mirror at Dakota. "Good! You ride, Dakota. Do you want to go riding with me tonight?"

Dakota stared at the back of his head. "Sure, that'd be fun."

Joshua turned his eyes back on the road. He liked her spunk. This would be fun. What a contrast between the two. Skye seemed all ladylike while Dakota took on the tomboy image. He was looking forward to getting to know both of them.

After the Sunday service, the people who were invited to the wedding stayed behind. Joshua was herded off into Pastor Ken's office while Angelina was kept in another room. Joshua felt nervous and wondered why. It was probably the fact that both sets of parents, his new sisters, and all his friends were there to witness their union.

"You look deep in thought, Joshua.

CHAPTER THIRTY

Care to share with me?" asked Ken, breaking the silence.

"I'm kind of nervous, Ken. Just thinking about all the people sitting out there, I guess."

"You're a pastor, Joshua. People shouldn't make you nervous."

Joshua thought about it for a few moments and replied, "You're right, Ken. I'll think about delivering a sermon instead of renewing my vows."

Ken smiled as he patted Joshua on the back. "By the way, when this day is over with, I want to hear about your experiences in Mexico."

"I was trying to get over to see you the other day, but I stopped at the Lindens first. I was there most of the afternoon. Ken, we will get together some time next week, okay?"

"I'll look forward to it, Joshua. Now let's go get you married again."

Joshua watched as Manuel walked with Angelina down the aisle. She was absolutely gorgeous. He would have to

WHEN TWO WORLDS COLLIDE

remember to thank his mom for her taste in dresses. The pale yellow accented Angelina's dark skin and she seemed to glow. Manuel looked very handsome too, in the new suit Dan had bought for him. Angelina and Manuel stood with Joshua at the front. After all the vows were spoken, Ken stood with the couple and their son. "Please help me welcome . . . Mr. and Mrs. Joshua Cole, and their son, Manuel."

Whistles and cheers sounded throughout the room. Joshua, Angelina and Manuel went outside and waited for the people to greet them. Hank Hurley was one of the first.

"Hank," said Joshua, surprised to see him. "I didn't know you were coming. I didn't even know how to get hold of you."

"I wouldn't have missed this celebration, Joshua. Angelina, you are beautiful. And Manuel, you did a fine job leading your mom down the aisle," spoke Hank in Spanish to Manuel.

"Gracias, Senor!"

Other people wanted the couple's attention so Hank started to walk away.

"You're coming to the ranch for the barbecue, aren't you, Hank?"

"Yes, I'm coming over with Mom and Dad. I'll see you later."

CHAPTER THIRTY

After greeting everyone, Angelina, Manuel and Joshua sat wearily in Joshua's truck.

"We're really married now, Angelina. You look so beautiful in the dress Mom bought you."

Angelina smiled sweetly. "Joshua, I pray we will always be kind to one another. The way you bless me with all your kind words make me want to burst inside. My prayer to God is that He will help me be a good wife and helper for you."

"Yes, Angelina. I pray the Lord will keep us walking in I Corinthians 13, the love chapter. We must work at it each day. I know the Lord will help us as we wait on Him. Could you also tell Manuel I want to be a good Papa to him, to love him and protect him?"

Angelina spoke softly to Manuel and his face lit up. "Can I call you Papa?"

Joshua laughed. "Manuel, your English is perfect. I would be honored if you called me Papa."

Manuel didn't understand all the words, so Angelina explained them to him.

"Well, we better get to our party," announced Joshua. "They'll be wondering where we are. Tonight we will be staying in our own home, Angelina. My aunt and uncle who were renting my place have since found their own."

"I'm so excited, Joshua. I can hardly wait to see it."

"If we had time, I would stop there now, but we'll see it later."

"Joshua, you have such a wonderful family. How do you like your new sisters?"

"Well," said Joshua pulling out of the church parking lot, "Dakota is sure rough around the edges and Skye seems really sweet. They sure are different from one another."

"I know. I met them one summer when I had an opportunity to go to Cochrane. Skye and I got along really well, but Dakota didn't want anything to do with me. I offered to go riding with her but she never wanted me to come. Guess she didn't think I could ride."

"You're an awesome rider, Angelina. I couldn't believe how you handled Blaze the other day. He sure behaved himself with you on his back. Have you had riding lessons before?"

"No, but I love to ride. Papa put me on a horse when I was younger than Manuel. He told me I'd better not fall off and I did-

CHAPTER THIRTY

n't, Joshua. I was more afraid of what Papa would do than the horse."

Joshua was careful to keep his eyes on the road as he put his arm around Angelina. "I won't let anyone hurt you like that again."

Angelina snuggled up to Joshua and closed her eyes. She silently thanked her Father in heaven for His goodness to her.

Later that same evening, Joshua pulled the truck into his yard. He noticed his uncle had kept the place in good condition. It actually looked better than when he had left it. Joshua, Angelina and Manuel stood on the porch. Joshua suddenly picked up Angelina in his arms and motioned for Manuel to open the door. Joshua carried Angelina into the house and put her down in the living room.

"Oh Joshua, this is wonderful! Look we have a fireplace and such wonderful windows to look out of. You can see the mountains from here. How beautiful!"

Joshua watched as Angelina went from room to room, her excitement rising with each discovery. Suddenly there was a squeal from Manuel as ran into one of the rooms. "Papa, is this my room?"

Joshua walked into the room and was just as surprised as Manuel. The room was tastefully decorated with articles for little boys. He would have to thank his mom later for all the work she did towards making this a wonderful homecoming for his new family. He left Manuel looking at all his new toys and went to find Angelina. There she was curled up on their four-poster bed, her eyes closed, breathing deeply. Joshua had wanted this night to be special, but knowing how tired Angelina had been, Joshua remembered they would have a lifetime of special nights together. He went back into Manuel's room and found some pajamas for him. After saying prayers, Joshua tucked him into bed and kissed his forehead. "Sleep well, my son."

Joshua wondered if he should do some reading but, after glancing at the mantle clock, he realized it was late. He had his work cut out for him tomorrow. The Shrivers would need a ride to the airport and he wanted to bring his stock back home. Joshua tiptoed into his room only to find Angelina missing. Two arms slipped around his waist as Angelina stood behind him.

CHAPTER THIRTY

"Do you think I would fall asleep on my wedding night, Mr. Cole?"

Joshua turned around and faced her. "I thought you were tired."

Angelina giggled, "Not anymore!"

Angelina and Joshua stood at the departure gate with the Shrivers.

"You will come and visit us, won't you Joshua?" Cynthia asked.

"We will drive up there soon, Cynthia. I'd love to see your place."

Doug looked serious as he drew Joshua to the side. "I'm really sorry for misleading you in Mexico, Joshua. Will you forgive us?"

"Doug, I do forgive you. I also would like to spend some time with you and your family to get to know them. God turned the situation around and only His blessings and goodness came out of the situation in Mexico. I'm really thankful it turned out this way. I love Angelina very much."

Doug hugged Joshua briefly and the two went back to where the girls were standing.

"Having a bonding time were you, Dad?" Dakota said sarcastically.

WHEN TWO WORLDS COLLIDE

Doug glared at Dakota and answered her sharply, "That'll be enough out of you, young lady. Don't be smart. I was just asking Joshua to forgive me for the ordeal I put him through in Mexico."

"Sorry, Dad. I didn't mean anything."

"Yes you did, or you wouldn't have said anything. Joshua isn't trying to take anyone's place in this family, but he is our son, and brother to you and Skye."

Soon the women of Doug's family were crying as the men and Angelina looked on. "I'm sorry, Dad, really," sniffed Dakota. "This is just new for us, having a brother and all."

Doug went over and put his arms around his daughter. "I know, so you must know how Joshua feels."

This hadn't really dawned on Dakota as she had thought only about her own feelings. She looked over at Joshua and smiled shyly. "Sorry, Joshua."

"Apology accepted." Joshua glanced at his watch. "You'd better go through customs. It's about that time."

After everyone hugged each other and the goodbyes were said, Angelina and Joshua left the airport.

"I guess we should plan a trip to see them one day. Manuel will like that," said

CHAPTER THIRTY

Joshua, driving to his aunt and uncle's place to return the van.

Angelina stifled a yawn and answered, "I would love to see Cochrane again. It's such a pretty town."

"Are you tired, Angelina?"

Angelina smiled. "We did have a pretty late night, Joshua."

Joshua smiled and squeezed her hand. "Yes, we did."

EPILOGUE

"Papa look at me!"

Joshua and Angelina stood at the rail fence and watched as Manuel rode his horse around the corral.

"Good, Manuel! Heels down . . . watch where you're going!" called Joshua proudly.

Joshua looked down at Angelina and her protruding stomach. Two more months and he would be a father again.

"You've taught him well, Joshua. And have you noticed his English pronunciation is getting better?"

"That's because you're such a good teacher, Angelina. I'm glad we decided to home-school him here in the States. It would be difficult for him to be in a regular school with our itinerary. Do you think he has too much of a workload going to school in Tijuana as well?"

"He's never complained Joshua. I think it's important for him to learn about the American culture as well as his own," said

Angelina, shifting her weight.

Joshua noticed this and took her hand. "Manuel, when you are finished riding, remember to brush the horse and put the tack away. Mom's tired, we're going to the house."

"I'm okay, Joshua. Please don't fuss over me. Let's watch Manuel for a few more minutes."

"A few minutes more then we're going to the house so I can rub your back. You look like you're hurting, are you?"

Angelina nodded. "The babies are active today. May be a nice back rub would help. Thank you, Joshua."

Joshua still couldn't believe they were having twins. Even though he remembered the vision his mom had had, it was still hard to comprehend. Having the babies born in the United States would give them dual citizenship, which would be beneficial for all concerned. The land left to Angelina had been turned into a mission for children. When the mission children were out of school, they would take them to the ranch to spend their holidays looking after the animals and working in the gardens. Joshua and Angelina worked closely with Martha's Mission. Thinking about his family,

EPILOGUE

Joshua lifted his face and began to praise and glorify God. He truly was a blessed man!

ABOUT THE AUTHOR

After 22 years of living and raising their family in Cochrane, Alberta, Barb and her husband, Fred, made their long-awaited move back to the country. Not far from their rural beginnings, the Engels purchased land east of Millet, Alberta, on Coal Lake. They named their 40 acre property 'Circle E Ranch', commemorating the journey that has taken them full circle back to their roots.

Barb has also written two other books and their titles are; *Darkness Exposed-- Passages From The Spirit* and *Stranger Within*. These books can be ordered from Barb by writing her at RR1, Millet, Alberta, Canada, T0C 1Z0. Her e-mail address is barbengels@myexcel.ca